THE HOUSE OF JESSE

Life-long Lessons from David and Goliath

by Perry Tuttle

Published by:
Provision One, Inc.
Charlotte, North Carolina

Produced by:
WESTMORELAND
Printers
Shelby, North Carolina

Overview

Many people have studied the life of David, but few have stopped to examine the influence of his father. David was known throughout his life as "the son of Jesse." Although he was the greatest king of Israel and, arguably, the greatest earthly king to ever reign, he was still known, even after death, as "the son of Jesse." Generations later, the Christ would be called not only a descendant of David, but as coming from "the root of Jesse." Who was this man who is mentioned by name seventeen times in I Samuel 16 and 17, while Goliath is named only three times? We all know the story of David and Goliath; what is Jesse's story? What clues does the Bible give us about his role as a father?

Ten key qualities are drawn from the Bible's earliest references to the House of Jesse in I Samuel 16 and 17. Each of these principles, from obedience to knowing how to give comfort, is amplified with stories from the author's life. A former professional football player who made the cover of *Sports Illustrated* as a college football star, Perry Tuttle weaves real life stories into the biblical text to bring the principles to life.

This book is directed towards fathers.

Table of Contents

Introduction

How It Began

It was 2:30 a.m. and I was face down on the floor, reading. For many years now I have set out a coffee cup and Bible before going to bed, trusting God to meet me if I awake during the night. The restless insomnia of my college football days has been replaced by expectation. God often speaks to me in the early morning hours.

I had quietly slipped out of bed, being careful not to wake Loretta, and then silently made my way downstairs to the study. As I opened my Bible I prayed, *"God, would you point me to your Word so that I can learn something today?"* For some reason I found myself turning to the old story of David and Goliath, wondering why I felt drawn to something I knew so well. Slowly, I began to make my way through I Samuel 16, the chapter before the fight.

The more I read, the more my attention became focused on Jesse, David's father. Over and over again his name was mentioned: eight times in the first eleven verses before David even came into the story. I had never noticed this before. Over the course of those two chapters, I Samuel 16 and 17, Jesse's name appeared seventeen times. Goliath was named only three times. I knew that repetition in the Bible doesn't occur by accident. For a man to be mentioned that many times was significant. *God*, I prayed, *what does this mean?*

In my imagination, I started to fill in the details of the house of Jesse. I wondered what sort of man he was. What did he look like? Was he old? Was he big? Did he have a beard? Was he black? What was his house like? Did his family eat around a table? As I began to daydream about Jesse, I mentally began to put my own boys in the story. I have six children including three sons; Jesse had eight sons.

I began to realize that hidden within the well-known story of David and Goliath is another story, a story for our generation. It's the story of a father whose influence is so profound that David was known throughout his life, even to its end, as "the son of Jesse" (II Samuel 23:1). Although David was the greatest king of Israel and, arguably, the greatest earthly king to ever reign, he was still known, even after death, as "the son of Jesse" (I Chronicles 29:6). Generations later, the Christ would be called not only a descendant of David, but as coming from "the root of Jesse" (Romans 15:12). Why was he so important? What could I learn from him about being a father?

Men, this story is for us. It's a story about how the world identifies us with our fathers. We are marked by them. But more importantly, it is a story about our house. It's a story that impresses upon the reader the powerful influence a father can have on his son. We can learn a lot from the house of Jesse. We can learn to become men with a reputation. We can learn to create the kind of house that is so significant that our boys—upon becoming men—will proudly say, "I am the son of this man; I was born into this man's house." As I have studied Jesse's house, I have identified ten aspects of David's upbringing that shaped the man he became. I'll share them with you in this book.

The World Asks Every Boy a Question

"Whose son are you, young man?"

After David killed Goliath, this was the only thing Saul wanted to know.

Earlier in the day, this same question was burning in Saul's thoughts as he watched young David make his way through the battle lines out to the field. Here was a kid who insisted he could whip Goliath. Saul had told him, "Don't be ridiculous! There is no way you can go against this Philistine. You are only a boy, and he has been in the army since he was a boy!" (I Samuel 17:33, NLT) David stood his ground and explained his reasons for why he believed he could win. Saul listened carefully, then relinquished. He granted him permission to fight. Now, as Saul stood on the hill and watched the boy work his way through the crowd of soldiers to reach Goliath, he turned to the commander of his army and asked,

"Abner, whose son is that young man?" His commander didn't know.

Perhaps Saul was thinking, "What kind of father raises a boy like that?" Here was a boy with a man's heart. He was ready to fight. He was prepared. Although Saul's camp was full of men—many of them experienced warriors—there wasn't one with the heart of a man. They were all scared and each one feared he would fail. This sad state of affairs had been underscored daily by Goliath. For forty days the Philistine had walked out onto the battlefield and shouted, "Give me a man!" Over and over again Saul's soldiers had heard this taunt: "Give me a man! *Give me a man!*" Saul didn't have one to give him. Not only were his men "terrified and deeply shaken" (I Samuel 17:11 NLT), but he was, too.

So now, here was David. No other man's son had stepped up like this boy. If this was the son, what was the father like? After David killed Goliath and walked back into the camp, Abner took him to Saul. Was David silent when he walked in before Saul—a young boy covered in blood, grasping the thick, matted hair of the dead warrior's head? Was he in that trance-like state that athletes experience after an all-consuming competition? David had been through an exhausting ordeal. Surely his heart pounded when he ran towards Goliath, preparing his sling. He shot a stone and Goliath fell face first into dust, a hundred-and-twenty-five pounds of bronze armor crashing with him. David kept running. He came up to Goliath, unconscious but still breathing, and dragged the oversized sword out of the scabbard. With only a kid's strength, he stood over the mighty warrior and brought the blade down on his neck. The head rolled off.

Now he stood before Saul holding the bloody prize.

As far as we know, Saul and David didn't discuss the fight. No words of congratulation were exchanged. The leaping and shouting on the battlefield were far away. In fact, an eerie quiet hangs over this scene. Saul had only one thing to say: Who's your daddy? *Tell me about your father,* I can imagine him saying, *because no other man's son acts like this.* How did you get that fight in you, boy? Who taught you that kind of fearlessness? Where did you learn such skill? *"Whose son are you, young man?"*

Why We Need to Answer That Question

Men, the world is going to ask our boys that question. We have the opportunity to answer it in advance by having a plan. So many men I talk to have carefully developed a business plan for their company. They may have a five-year plan, a ten-year plan, and even a plan for how they will pass the company down to the next generation. They've studied the numbers, talked to the accountant, evaluated the market and sized up the competition. But how many fathers have developed a business plan for their sons? I don't mean a financial plan, but a plan for how they will develop, nurture, and guide their sons into manhood? What an incredible opportunity we have to prepare our boys for life. This preparation will not only distinguish them, but it will answer the question, "Whose son are you?" We are the answer to that question. How we answer it is what this book is about.

As I studied David's interactions with Jesse and how he conducted himself at home, on the battlefield, around grown men, and in Saul's court, certain characteristics became clear. I saw qualities I wanted for my own children. David was obedient. What Jesse asked him to do, he did. He was responsible because he could be trusted to carry out a request. David was capable, indicating that someone had provided him with solid instruction about life. He shared his talents, using his natural abilities in music to give comfort to a troubled king. He had insight and wasn't influenced by outward appearances. He was able to look past Goliath and see larger issues. He was also spiritually minded, for he knew a champion wasn't defined by events but by friendship with God. And when he left his father, he returned to his father. He had a home worth coming back to.

David, the son of Jesse, learned some valuable lessons at home.

In this book we will look closely at those lessons. I'm excited that you are here and I am praying that your love for your son will deepen through these pages. Thanks for joining me.

Chapter 1

....

Fathers, Teach Your Sons
Not To Look On Outward Appearances

"But the Lord said to Samuel, 'Do not consider his appearance or his height, for I have rejected him. The Lord does not look at the things man looks at. Man looks at the outward appearance, but the Lord looks at the heart.'" I Samuel 16: 7, NIV

David, the Misjudged Son

Samuel, a prophet of God, was on a secret mission. The man he had anointed king over Israel, Saul, was turning out to be a failure. An impressive and tall young man who had shown much promise, Saul was a king who valued outward appearances. He preferred looking right to being right. When he did something wrong, he justified himself. When pressured, he compromised.

God sent Samuel to the house of Jesse to anoint another king. Jesse had eight sons, but he only presented seven to the revered prophet. Even David's own father misjudged him. It was not until Samuel had rejected the others that Jesse sent out to the fields for his youngest. This must have been a life-changing experience for David. Every one of his brothers was invited to attend a religious ceremony with the most famous prophet of the day. David was not considered important enough to be there.

Samuel, also, had his prejudices. When he saw Jesse's firstborn son, Eliab, he immediately jumped to the conclusion that this was the future king. We can speculate from God's remark to Samuel ("'Do not consider his appearance or his height,'" I Samuel 16:7) that Eliab was handsome and tall. Ironically, so was King Saul. Was Samuel looking for a king like him? God chastened the prophet with these words: "The Lord does not look on the things man looks at. Man looks at the outward appearance, but the Lord looks at the heart'" (I Samuel 16:7).

What Samuel could not see was Eliab's heart. Although the Bible does not tell us much about him, we learn something of his character in the next chapter. In fact, David's oldest brother could serve as an example of the kind of son who could give a father heartache. When David showed up at the military encampment and started asking questions about Goliath, Eliab became furious. He accused David of being conceited and of having a wicked heart—strong words, especially from an older brother. He deeply misjudged David, perhaps out of jealousy. He was suspicious, accusing, judgmental, harsh, condescending and unloving. The man who seemed a good choice to the prophet Samuel because of his outward appearance would have been a miserable choice if chosen by the standard of his character, insight, and good judgment.

The World Our Boys Live In

Every day our children operate in a world that places value on the way things look. Whether it's name brand jeans, a certain style of shoe, the house a friend lives in, a cell phone or computer game, impressions are seductive. Our children are constantly pressured to form opinions based on outward appearances.

Appearances can be misleading.

I went to Clemson on a football scholarship and got a lot of playing time my freshman year. My sophomore year I was scheduled to start with the team. I was confident and excited. Until a rumor began to circulate.

Word got around that a new receiver was being transferred to our school. A few days after the talk started, this guy showed up. I couldn't believe it. He was chiseled—everything about his body told me he was the perfect receiver. He was slim but not skinny; he had that receiver strut. And the dude was handsome. If you put together the good looks of Jerry Rice and Lynn Swann, you'd have a good idea of what this guy looked like.

That whole summer, as the team worked out, I watched him. He became my unspoken competition because of his outward appearance. What he had, I wanted. When I looked at him I silently thought, "I wish . . . I wish . . ." Everything about him—who he was, what he looked like, what he had—magnified my flaws.

Until training camp began. In the first two or three days of camp, the truth about him was suddenly revealed. He couldn't catch a cold. He was absolutely terrible. Eventually, he ended up leaving the team.

One guy, just by his outward appearance, had completely shaken my confidence in myself. One Goliath, completely by his outward appearance, shook the confidence of an army. But in my case, the problem wasn't the guy, the problem was me. I wasn't secure in what my game was about; I defined myself by someone else. This is what happens when our focus is on the externals. It's a mistake anyone can make, even a godly man like Samuel who has walked many years with the Lord.

A boy's family can teach him a lot about judging others. David probably learned how to avoid guys like his older brother Eliab. My older brother taught me a lesson about outward appearances, but it was one that drew me to him, and to guys like him.

Eddie, My Misjudged Brother

The first time I played on a sports team I was in fourth grade. That fall, in our small North Carolina town, I joined the football team at our school. Our coach was a man who would have a big impact on my life.

Coach Pete Chitty was a short man, about the same height as my dad, but in every other way he was unlike my father. He was white, prematurely balding, and always seemed to be having so much fun. He laughed a lot. He saw something more in me than what others saw, especially my third grade teacher. Just a few days before third grade was to end, Mrs. Gatewood pulled me aside on the playground to tell me I had flunked third grade. We were standing near a wall and it was recess. I remember being stunned, and just leaning against the wall. She informed me that she and the principal believed I would have a better chance if I were placed in "the special class." She had already talked to my mom.

I stared at the kids on the playground and thought about the special class. Those kids didn't get to play sports.

Most of the kids in the special class had Downs Syndrome. We called them retarded. Even though I was only eight, I knew I wasn't one of those kids. I knew I wasn't like them because my best friend, my older brother Eddie, was in that class. Their facial expressions were different—they smiled a lot—and when they talked, they were loud. They rode a separate bus. I saw these students every day at school behave in unpredictable ways. They meant no harm, their behavior was just random. They were never allowed to play football or any other organized sport. The way they ran was different. The way they walked was different.

I saw how the other kids judged my brother. They laughed at his awkward appearance. Eddie was short, his eyes bulged and were often red. It was hard to understand what he said. Those who only saw his physical appearance never got close enough to see the heart I saw.

I wish every little boy could have a friend like Eddie. He was my first hero. He didn't think carefully enough about things to be afraid. When Luke, the school bully, whipped me, the next day Eddie went out and beat him up. For a black kid growing up in a small Southern town, that was heroic. Eddie stood up for me.

As I grew up, my brother became a cheerleader without equal. No matter what I did, if I fumbled a ball or made a touchdown, Eddie was there to praise me. He would find a place to sit right behind the bench, usually coming an hour before the game. He would get there early, when the team was warming up, just to see me. During the game I could hear him shouting in his garbled voice, "Gooooooo Pooweeee." That was the best he could manage for "Perry." Although it was difficult to understand his speech, it wasn't hard to understand his heart.

Sometimes the people who are the most unlike us, or of

little importance to the world, are the ones who give us the things we need most.

Eddie gave me support. His love for me was unconditional. He accepted me in a way that wasn't qualified by my performance. He cheered me on.

When Eddie died in a hospital in 1999, after several difficult years in a wheelchair, I thought about two other things he had given me.

Eddie gave me perspective. Once, when we were adults, I came into a room where Eddie was hanging out with some of his friends. I saw that they were laughing and talking among themselves on one side of the room while pointing at me. This was a strange feeling. Later, I asked Eddie what they were laughing at. "You," he said, with no embarrassment or apologies. It dawned on me how different our worlds were. I had grown up seeing "normal" people laugh and point at people with Downs Syndrome. In a normal world, they didn't fit. But in Eddie's world, I didn't fit. His friends were just as amused by my uptight anxiety and impatience as normal people were amused by the awkward movements and facial expressions of the kids with Downs.

Eddie also gave me perspective on winning. Eddie loved to run, and although it became more difficult for him as he grew older, he was able to compete and do well in the Special Olympics. As a kid, he ran like a Tasmanian devil, yelling and arms flying in every direction. He flustered the other kids so badly during sandlot football games that they would wait for him to run past before trying to tackle him. There were just too many limbs going in too many directions to risk a head-on tackle.

Eddie loved to run, and he continued to run during his twenties in the Special Olympics. He won a number of trophies, including ones for the hundred-yard-dash and the long jump. One of his favorites was the relay. But I never got used to his way of doing it. In the Special Olympics, a runner comes to a stop before handing off the baton. The new runner takes it and starts running. But in Eddie's case, if his team was ahead, he would wait for the competitors to catch up so that he could have a really good race. Although I would shout from the sidelines, "Eddie, RUN!" no amount of yelling would convince Eddie to get going. He wanted to race. He wanted to win. If the other team was ahead, he would catch up. If they were behind, he would wait. Eddie gave me perspective on the joy of competing, on the thrill of the race.

The other thing Eddie gave me was hope. Sometimes it's hard to tell what a person really believes. This can be especially true of those who can't communicate well. One afternoon when my wife Loretta and I were at a Carolina Panthers' football game in Charlotte, we got a call to come home to Winston-Salem. "Eddie's not going to make it through the night," we were told. My heart was heavy, and I wanted to talk to Eddie one last time about the gospel. Was it clear to him? Did he understand the hope he had?

There in the hospital room I talked to my brother about God the Father and his relationship to Jesus Christ the Son. "Eddie, do you see Daddy?" I asked, pointing to our father. "We're his sons," I continued. I explained those precious truths one last time. When I finished, I asked my brother, "Eddie, where is God?" Eddie pointed to the ceiling. I took a breath then asked the tough question. "Eddie, where is Jesus?" With that Eddie pointed to his heart. I looked at my brother for one of the last times here on earth. Overcome with emotion, I told him, "Eddie, the day that I die, I'm going to be looking into Jesus' face, and he will hug me, but I am going to be looking over his shoulder for you." It was an eternity moment. Eddie and I knew we would be together again.

Fathers, Set Your Sons Free

As men, we know that our boys will be tempted all of their lives to live by outward appearances. The same thing that happened to me my sophomore year at Clemson—a version of it—will happen to your son. He will be tempted to define himself by what others appear to have. Life will become an exercise of completing the sentence that begins with "I wish . . ." Daddy, you can set your son free from this bondage by teaching him to look up. We know from the Psalms that David defined himself by God's opinion of him. We can teach our sons to do the same.

Our boys will also face what the prophet Samuel experienced: They'll be tempted to believe a handsome exterior holds an attractive interior. Or worse, that a great-looking exterior is all that matters.

Or our boys will be tempted—like the people who never took a better look at my brother Eddie—to think that some people have worth and others don't. Show your sons by example that in Christ we are free to love all kinds of people.

Life will present you with many opportunities to teach your son. Take advantage of them. Speak about them. The heart of the matter doesn't stand in an obvious place. Rarely is it found at first glance. Seeing beyond appearances requires patience and insight. Without these qualities we fall for what we see on the exterior, for the shiny gold things, the superficial things. When the people of Troy accepted the colossal wooden horse from the Greeks, they had no idea that it was a trap. They thought they were getting a gift, but the enemy was inside. If you've let a Trojan horse into your life, tell your son about it. Share your life experiences that have taught you the disastrous results of believing outward appearances. Then look for illustrations in your son's everyday life that reveal this truth. Teach him to ask questions that take him deeper, that take him to the heart.

Chapter 2

....

Fathers, Teach Your Sons To Be Obedient

"Jesse's three oldest sons had followed Saul to the war. . . . but David went back and forth from Saul to tend his father's sheep at Bethlehem." I Samuel 17: 13, 15, NIV

David Makes a Choice

Every young boy wants to fight. It's a natural desire. He wants to get in the battle and see what he's made of. He wants a challenge. As he grows into a man, the desire to fight gets bigger. He wants to fight for his country, for his wife, for his kids. The desire to fight is a natural instinct in a man, and if it's not put to the test in war, it will look for a challenge in other places. That's why men love sports. It's not just about skill, it's about beating someone.

I try to imagine how difficult it was for young David to obey his father. He knew there was a war going on, but unlike his brothers who got to join the army, he had to stay home and take care of the livestock. His dad sent him back and forth between the fields of Bethlehem and the army base fifteen miles away. David would deliver food to his brothers, then head back home. I wonder what it was like for him to walk away from a fight, hearing the sounds fade in the distance. As long as Saul was king, there was fighting between his men and the Philistines (I Samuel 14:52).

David's father at this time was old. The Bible says Jesse was "well advanced in years" (I Samuel 17:12). David faithfully left the battle encampment time and again to return home and help his elderly father. He took care of the sheep, which weren't many if we take literally a sarcastic comment by his oldest brother ("And with whom did you leave those few sheep in the desert?" I Samuel 17:28). It was a low job. But we know the boy was a fighter because of what he later said to Saul when pressing for a chance to fight Goliath. "When a lion or a bear came and carried off a sheep from the flock, I went after it," he said. "When it turned on me, I seized it by its hair, struck it and killed it" (I Samuel 17:35). He killed to protect his sheep, even when it meant going in at close range. Can you imagine going after a lion with perhaps nothing more than a slingshot? Of being so close in a fight that you can feel its breath? Of grabbing it by the mane? Of feeling its powerful legs come against you? A lion is raw power with an instinct to kill. David didn't back down. With seven older brothers at home, there must have been a lot of scrapping. Maybe David grew up swinging.

He was not rash. His passion was tempered by obedience. As I study his interactions with Jesse, I see a son who was obedient to his father. In the years ahead this would bear fruit, often yielding a spirit of self-control. When given the opportunity to kill Saul, a man who was trying to kill him or have him killed, he resisted. When given the chance to seize power for himself, he walked away. In most circumstances he was not willing to seize control. He waited upon God to give to him. His obedience opened the door to wisdom, something his son Solomon mentions frequently in Proverbs.

Opportunity Knocks

I know the power of obedience because early in my pro-football career I took a wide turn down the path of disobedience. At the time I felt justified, but the consequences have affected me for decades.

It was the summer of 1982 and I was upstairs in a large, new house in a white neighborhood. I wanted to buy my mom a home and I had picked a white neighborhood hoping that my dad—the most prejudiced man I had ever known—would stay away. He didn't. He had come along that day with my mom, me, a real estate agent, and the sports agent who was courting me to sign with him. I was alone upstairs with my dad and the others were downstairs. Although it was morning, I could smell the beer on his breath. He was an alcoholic and hard to live with; there were times when he'd come home and throw everyone out of the house—my mom included. I had no desire to give him a home.

My career at Clemson was finished and I was getting ready to go pro. I was All American and my photograph had been on the cover of *Sports Illustrated* with the headline, "Orange Bowl Hero Perry Tuttle of Clemson." I was the nineteenth draft pick in the nation. I was seeing my value. I was the hero in my neighborhood—kids were wearing orange jerseys with "22" on the front and "Tuttle" on the back. I had a future that promised millions of dollars. I was *the man*.

Upstairs my dad turned to me and spoke about the sports agent downstairs. With remarkable clarity he said, "Don't you sign with that man. He's a crook. He'll take everything you've got." He spoke with authority.

I was stunned. Anger burned in me. My dad had done nothing to help me and had taken no interest in my career. In all the years that I played football, he had only been to one of my games. And here he was telling me how to go pro? What did he know about the sports agent who was downstairs? The man was well known in the pro community and had a reputation for getting the money. He was a smart attorney from California and my dad was a nobody who didn't have an education and who didn't take care of things.

"What do you know?" I said with contempt. "Shut up."

I signed with the agent.

Disobedience Catches Up With Us

Three years later I was on my first official date with Loretta. We were at a fine restaurant with another couple and a mutual friend. The bill came and I said, "I'll take care of it." I enjoyed having the wealth to be generous. I was living the life of my dreams: driving the car I wanted to drive, living where I wanted, buying what I wanted, doing what I wanted. I slipped my credit card inside the folder.

A few minutes later the waiter returned to the table. "Sir, would you come with me?" he asked. I walked with him up to the front desk and watched in shock as he cut up my credit card in front of me. What was going on? Unknown to me, the credit card company gave a bonus to people who cut the cards of deadbeat clients. I tried calling my agent but couldn't get him. Embarrassed, I went back to the table, unable to pay the bill. Nothing like this had ever happened to me before.

This was only the beginning. Over the next several years one disclosure followed another as I learned how this agent had mismanaged my affairs. Money that was designated for investments was squandered on dubious ventures, including a horse farm owned by one of his family members. I thought the $1.6 million I had earned was growing, but it was really disappearing. I had foolishly given this man power of attorney over all of my financial affairs. Taxes I thought were being paid weren't. Big holes were developing in my portfolio. By 1990 I found myself in court in California, not only without funds, but facing a debt of $300,000. A loan the agent took out in my name had defaulted and the bank that approved the loan was taken over by the FDIC during the savings and loan debacle. Loretta and I had been married two years and she was pregnant with our first child. The FDIC wanted their money.

God was gracious. The brother of another pro-athlete agreed to represent me after two law firms turned me down. My situation didn't look promising, yet he took my case for free. He knew what a crook this agent was because he had taken his brother through the cleaners several years earlier. We won our case and the agent was disbarred. But it was a costly lesson in disobedience. I learned that the fruit of disobedience may take years to ripen before the full consequences of it come to light.

God Doesn't Leave Us Hanging

The good news is that God uses our disobedience to change us. We learn through the things we suffer to become better sons.

My father died in 2000 as a man of faith. The last eight years of his life he lived for Christ. We talked almost every day. Apart from my wife, he became the single most important person in my life.

One day we were talking and I found the courage to say something that had been weighing on me for years. "Dad, do you remember the day we were buying this house?" I began. "I need to ask your forgiveness . . . "

My father dropped his head. Tears were running down his face, not small tears or streams of tears, but big, great drops of tears that fell and splashed on the table. I had only begun to say what was on my heart. As I continued to apologize for the words I spoke many years ago, I saw how deeply I had wounded him. All those years my words had troubled my conscience and been a burden; now I saw that they had pierced my father's heart, too. We made things right that day and I think it was the best day of my life. Shortly after that he died.

I don't know how to explain this, but it was almost like my father, by forgiving and affirming me, put a launching pad under my life that day. I had been growing as a Christian, yes, but after that my life took a significant turn. If growing could make a sound, it became deafening. There was a breakthrough.

Obedient Fathers Will Teach Their Sons Obedience

Parenthood is tough. As my children get older they see my flaws. Obedience becomes tougher. In the same way that I questioned my father, they also think, "Does he really know what he's talking about?" Obedience requires faith: They must choose to believe that I truly have their best interests at heart and that they can trust me. A godly father's faithfulness is a picture to them of our heavenly Father's care. We can obey God because we know He cares for us and has our best interests at heart. Our faith makes obedience possible. Paul wrote about this in his letter to the believers in Rome. He explained to his spiritual children that as an apostle, his job was "to call people from among all the Gentiles to the obedience that comes from faith" (Romans 1:5, NIV). Likewise, we call our children to an obedience that comes from faith.

Paint a Picture For Your Sons

Two years ago my oldest son, Korde, and I were in our car on the way to a ball game. He was thirteen years old. I was talking to him about obedience. It was a serious conversation.

"Korde," I asked, "would you obey me even if you didn't understand what I was asking of you?"

"Yes," he said. I pressed him on it. "Do you trust me, Korde? Do you really believe I will do what is best for you?" "Yes," he insisted. He assured me he would obey me. The next day I decided to test him. I wanted to give him a picture that would stay in his mind about the rewards of obedience. So I got out the castor oil.

Korde was upstairs in his room and I knocked and went in. I announced I had some medicine I wanted him to take. I don't know if you have ever smelled castor oil, but it's pretty bad stuff. If you've seen it in the old cartoons, you know it can send kids running. So I gave Korde a whiff of the castor oil. I held a spoon in the other hand, full of glistening liquid. He looked at me in distress. He started objecting. "Dad," he said, "I feel okay."

"Korde, yesterday you told me you would obey me, even if you didn't understand what I was asking of you. You said you trusted me—that you knew I would never ask anything of you that would harm you. I want you to swallow this," I said. This went on for awhile as I pressed Korde to understand that what he says has to line up with what he does. If he said he would obey me, even when it seemed I was asking something unreasonable of him, then he needed to be obedient.

At last Korde opened his mouth. To his amazement the spoonful of liquid was sweet. I had secretly loaded the spoon with honey before I came upstairs. My son went from tears to smiles. What he expected was something that would be sour, bitter. What he got was sweet. It was a picture of the spiritual truth of obedience. It may seem like God is asking us to swallow a bitter pill when we obey Him, but when we surrender it becomes sweet to our taste.

Hold the Line

It's tempting, as fathers, to compromise. I've seen many parents make concessions when teaching their children to obey them. It often starts early with a very bad habit: counting. A mom or dad will give their child an order and when the child doesn't obey, they start making threats. "I mean what I said!" they will say, usually in frustration. "You had better mind me right now! I'm going to count and you had better not be standing on that couch by the time I get to three!" If the child is slow to respond, the parent may drag out the counting to give more time. Instead of "one" it becomes "o . . . n . . . e . . ."

Dads, this is no way to teach our children to be obedient. It is teaching them to negotiate at a young age. You are actively training your son to not take you seriously. Don't fail him like this. Hold the line and teach him to be obedient the first time. You'll both be glad you did when he's a man.

We have no control over whether our sons choose faith, which is at the core of all true obedience. It's at the core of our own obedience to God. But we do have control over whether we raise them in God's ways. As I have told Korde, who is now fifteen and in high school, "If you choose to walk away from the faith and you have dreadlocks and wear an earring and move to New Orleans (I actually said that before Katrina), and you don't want to have anything to do with Daddy, I will love you just as much. If you do things that I disagree with, I am still going to love you. But obedience is what *you choose*; it's what you do with what you hear. I will not be a guilty father who didn't show you the way to go. I will do what God requires of me. Your mother and I will not spend our days looking at each other and saying, 'Where did we go wrong?' We are going to teach you the way that is best for you.

"Korde, if you stay pure, sexually pure, and you remain committed academically, then I promise you God will bless you with a godly woman. He will bless you academically if you will do what's right. If you're obedient it always pays off," I have told him.

We need to tell our sons—with our words—what their future looks like if they will walk with God. The "silence of Adam" is not good enough. They need to hear our words, encouraging them to be obedient. We must speak up. We must give them a preview of the future. That's what Coach Pete Chitty did for me.

Give Your Son a Vision of the Future

When I was in the fourth grade, Coach Pete was driving me home from practice one day because I didn't have a ride. We were in the car—I'm just a young kid with a big helmet on, these awkward shoulder pads, big football pants and my number twenty-two jersey—and Coach Pete puts his hand on my knee and says, "Perry, if you keep working at it, one day you're going to play in the NFL." He spoke life into me. In that moment, he gave me a vision of what I could be. He gave me a dream that I could follow. I became obedient to that vision.

Because of that, I would literally get out in my backyard and pretend I was in a stadium; I would daydream about thousands of people watching this game being played. I would take an old football and imagine that one moment I'm the quarterback and one moment I'm the receiver. The coach sends me in.

I played this game all by myself. And I worked at it. When I was in college I would lie in my bed at night, on my back with the lights on, and toss the football to the ceiling and catch it a hundred times. My roommate thought I was crazy. Then I would turn out the lights and do a hundred times in the dark. The first time I started doing it in the dark, the ball would hit me upside the head. But the more I did it, the better I got. In the dark the ball became a part of me; I could catch it, feel it, smell the leather. Because I practiced in the dark so many times I came to believe that if a ball touched my hands in a football game, I was going to catch it.

Because Coach Pete spoke into my life, I was motivated to try to excel. I was also tested.

My freshman year I actually quit for a day. During training camp the coach changed my position from receiver to defensive back. Because I had such a dream of catching the winning touchdown, I quit. I knew I was meant to be a receiver. I decided to find a team that would let me play that position. Quietly, I packed up my room and drove back to my home town. It wasn't easy; I was discouraged. Later, when it worked out for me to return to Clemson as a receiver, I learned a valuable lesson: Hold on to your dream.

Dads, we need to give our sons a vision of the dream we have for them, not about football, but about being a man after God's own heart, a man like David. We need to speak words of life into their hearts, describing what we see for them in the years to come. The imagination is a powerful instrument; use it to fire your son's vision for the man he can become. Teach him to be obedient to the calling God has on his life. Use stories from your own life to illustrate both the fruits of obedience and the hardship of disobedience. You've got a treasury of life lessons that you can share with him to explain what it means to obey from the heart.

Tell him about David and of how he stayed home with the sheep when his brothers got to fight. One day his chance came. By being obedient he learned to fight the lion and the bear, gaining the confidence and skills he would one day need to kill a giant. He didn't know Goliath was in his future, all he knew was that the lion and the bear were in his present. If he had rushed into the army against his father's wishes, we would have never heard the story of David and Goliath. His future victory depended on remaining obedient in the present.

Chapter 3

....

Fathers, Encourage Your Sons
To Give Comfort

"I have seen a son of Jesse of Bethlehem who knows how to play the harp . . . . And the Lord is with him." I Samuel 16:18

David's Gift Breaks Through Darkness

Saul was a troubled man. After lying to the prophet Samuel about his disobedience to God, a change came over him. The Bible says that the Spirit of the Lord left him and an evil spirit began to torment him. Even his attendants noticed a change. The situation was disturbing.

As Saul's servants watched him slip into darkness, they wondered what they could do. Knowing the soothing effects of music, they came up with an idea: Why not look for a harp player? Perhaps music would have a calming effect on the king. They asked Saul for permission to search for someone who could play the harp. "You will feel better," they assured him.

These men knew that Saul wasn't just going through a period of depression. They saw his condition as a spiritual problem. Saul's mood shift wasn't due to discouragement, but to the presence of an evil spirit. Although this may be hard for our modern minds to grasp, the Bible presents it as a matter of fact. That's why the men who took care of Saul knew they had to do more than find a good harp player. They needed someone who would bring the presence of God to Saul.

One of the men spoke to the king. He never mentioned David's name, only Jesse of Bethlehem. "I have seen a son of Jesse of Bethlehem who knows how to play the harp," he began. He described David as good-looking and well spoken. "He is a brave man and a warrior," the servant told the king. "And the Lord is with him."

This plan appealed to Saul, so he sent a messenger to Jesse. We don't know what Jesse said or how he may have counseled David, only that he "took a donkey loaded with bread, a skin of wine and a young goat and sent them with his son David to Saul" (verse 20). Saul asked for David's services and Jesse made the arrangements.

The king liked the young man. David's harp playing brought peace to the troubled ruler. "Whenever the spirit from God came upon Saul, David would take his harp and play. Then relief would come to Saul; he would feel better, and the evil spirit would leave him" (verse 23). Because God was with David, his talents deeply affected others. David's talent opened doors, but God's Spirit transformed his talent into ministry.

Giving Comfort Is About God In Us

So many times we fall for the lie that our talents make us great. Our talents don't make us great; God in us makes us great. David was able to help Saul because God was with him. David learned to play the harp and was a skillful player, but skill alone did not meet Saul's heart need. To truly comfort someone requires not only our natural talent, but also God's presence in us. The Holy Spirit works through our natural abilities to supernaturally bring comfort to others.

Raw talent isn't enough. Look at all of the people who have accomplished important things, then ask yourself the question: How many of them understand how to use their talents to care about others? The answer, sadly, is very few. It's not enough to be talented; you need to be abiding in Christ. When we commit our talents to Him, He opens our eyes to see how we can genuinely bring comfort to others. God sees things we can't naturally see or understand. Through our relationship with Him, we gain insight that takes us beyond the obvious, giving us practical ideas or meaningful words to touch a heart. It's a matter of the heart, not the head.

For one man, it was a matter of the feet.

Comfort From the Bottom Up

Young Stephen Crotts stood on the porch of the small mill home and knocked. Just a few years out of seminary, he was pastoring a congregation in a North Carolina town not far from where I grew up. Tonight he had been called to the home of a woman whose husband had suddenly died. Stephen shifted his weight as he glanced at the peeling paint, then the nearby railroad tracks. He didn't know this elderly woman very well, but she was faithful at church.

When the door opened he was surprised to see a room full of people. Looking weary and strained, Wilma remained seated as he walked in to greet her.

"I didn't come to visit," he explained, looking into her tired eyes. "I came to offer my sympathy. We'll get through this together," he reassured her. They spoke a few minutes and then another knock sounded at the door.

An older man entered the room, a mill worker who had clearly just gotten off a shift. His shirt was marked with perspiration; lint clung to his short hair. Wearing steel-toed boots, he made his way to Wilma. Gently taking both of her hands, he looked straight and steady into her eyes and quietly said, "Wilma, you have my deepest sympathy." He paused. "I came to get your shoes. I'll make them up nice for you, for tomorrow."

Wilma had grandchildren who were young. Soon a paper grocery bag was filled with worn leather shoes of all sizes. The bag was handed to the man and he quietly turned and left. Crotts didn't recognize him from church. "Must be a neighbor," he thought to himself.

That night in 1978, Stephen Crotts caught a glimpse of a humble heart that knew the meaning of comfort. It transformed him. Driving home that night he prayed, "Lord, I don't want to be a great preacher, to be rich or well-educated or even famous. I just want to be a good lover like that mill worker who knows how to polish shoes."

When the family put on their Sunday best for the funeral, their shoes were gleaming. Their hearts were strengthened and comforted by this unassuming gift. It didn't cost much and it wasn't showy, but it brought them assurance that someone cared. It was a gift of comfort.

Use What You Have

Dads, our boys need to use what they have. David liked to play a harp. He wasn't seeking greatness, he was just doing something that gave him pleasure. It was his gift.

Like Jesse, we need to bless our sons as they develop their gifts. How did David learn to play the harp? We don't know. What we do know is that Jesse blessed David when his gift was needed. The Bible says that Jesse prepared David to go to King Saul. David didn't go to the stable to get the donkey and the goat; the Bible says that Jesse did. He loaded up the donkey with bread and wine, then slipped a rope over a young goat's neck and tied it to the donkey. Jesse sent his son off; he sent him with a blessing.

David's gift took him away from his father, but we don't see Jesse holding on. Jesse was an old man who needed his son's help with the livestock. He was losing a reliable son. But he didn't hold David back; instead, he blessed him and sent him out. Playing a harp may not have seemed like a lot, but David did it well. Growing up in the House of Jesse, David learned to use what he had.

Our boys need our encouragement to look around and see what they have that can bring comfort to others. It may be a gift of music or the ability to make others laugh. It could be mowing a lawn or feeding the neighbors' dogs. Comfort comes in many forms. It can even be shaped like a baseball.

Small Things Matter

I have a friend who loves baseball. Over twenty years ago he lived in Greenville, South Carolina, a city that was the AA affiliate for the Atlanta Braves. He loved taking his young son to the Greenville games. Because Atlanta was only a couple of hours away, they occasionally drove to Fulton County Stadium to watch the Braves play.

When his son, Philip, was six, one of his playmates—a little boy named Frank—was diagnosed with a brain tumor. The family was devastated, and the boy's condition quickly worsened. My friend struggled to help his son understand what was going on. As he talked to him about what they could do for the sick child, they came up with an idea. Philip had a very special baseball his dad had given him that was signed by the entire Atlanta Braves team. He would take that to Frank.

The family later told them that little Frank slept with the coveted baseball the last weeks before his death. The baseball became his treasured possession. It told him something that words aren't big enough to tell a kid: that he was worthy of receiving a gift of great value. Frank knew, in receiving a treasure most boys only dream of, that he was significant. We are comforted when we are reassured that we have not been forgotten or overlooked. When someone makes a sacrifice on our behalf, we are comforted in ways that are bigger than words.

The baseball was a special gift, but God loves to take things that are simple or insignificant to bring comfort to others. When Hurricane Katrina hit the Gulf in 2005, one of the biggest messes that had to be fixed was the plumbing. We will probably never know how many humble, godly plumbers took vacation time to go to Louisiana, Mississippi, and Alabama. People are comforted when someone offers help in the midst of an overwhelming need. My friend, Tom, has been learning about that.

Breakdowns Are Opportunities

Tom is head of maintenance for a large hospital and he has an unusual gift. He can fix just about anything. It doesn't matter what it is; Tom can figure out how it works. For years I have told him that he is probably the most talented man I have ever met. He can build anything you want—including computers and other electrical and mechanical things. I call him sometimes when I get in a jam. Me, and a lot of other people.

One day we were standing in a parking lot talking about friendship. He looked at me and said, "Why don't I have friends?" He wanted to understand why he couldn't go deeper with other men. "I feel used," he admitted. "People call me when they want something fixed. Even you, Perry. You only call me when you need something fixed. I just want to have a friend."

I asked his forgiveness. We continued to talk about talents, and why we have them. God's glory is the backdrop of all that we do, especially what we do with our talents. "Tom," I explained, "you don't know how attractive your talent is to another man. What you need to do when someone calls you is to expand that into friendship. Take it outside of a hammer and wires and move it into friendship."

As I stood there thinking about how our talents give us the opportunity to bring comfort to others, I made a connection. Tom had invited me a few days earlier to go to a pro football game with him and his son. They were estranged, and it had been ten years since he had seen him. Now a young man, he had become a big fan of the Atlanta Falcons, a team I used to play on. "Tom, let me tell you the reason why you called me, after so many months. Your son loves the Falcons and the only guy you know that can connect with your son is someone with my talents. Now if your son wanted to go to a truck show down at the coliseum, guess who never would have gotten called? So you leaned on me, based on what you knew about me, for God's glory. You knew that I could connect with your son. Your desire is for your son. Because he's unsaved, you want me to speak into his life. Now, if he had no interest at all in football, if he just wanted to go to a truck show, there would have been some other man you would have connected with to bring into his life." He had to smile.

Our talents make us attractive to others, giving us an opportunity—for God's glory—to bring comfort into their lives. If we've been through a lot of rejection in life, it may take awhile to see that we're not being used by others, but that God is opening doors for us to glorify Him. Don't let others define the use of your gifts for the glory of God. You will feel either used or undervalued if you do.

How to Identify and Develop Your Son's Gifts

Talents often need silence and isolation to develop. David probably spent many long hours outdoors on his own. In that isolated setting—marked by silence—he picked up a harp.

He was also working. Taking care of sheep was considered a menial task, not a poetic assignment. David did not live in a child-oriented culture, but in a family-oriented culture. He learned to play a harp while fulfilling his responsibilities to his family. This is an important issue for us. Dads, I would encourage you not to make your kids the center of your family. Not only is that unhealthy for your marriage, but it is bad for your kids. Encourage their talents to develop within healthy boundaries. Teaching our boys to play sports is a great thing, but teaching them responsibilities within the family is even greater. If they can pick up a fumble, they can pick up their clothes.

To help your son develop, get to know and understand his personality, his unique bent in life. Be willing to bend yourself, in order to give him the room he needs to grow. I know of a family with seven children, ages 11 to 22, and their handsome boys are very athletic. The two oldest are attending colleges on athletic scholarships but the youngest son has shown promise in an unusual area. He's a dancer who has drawn national attention from some of the finest dancers in America. Young Silas has taken some ribbing from his older brothers, but his parents have given him the space he needs to develop what's inside. If the father had been all about football, he would have crushed Silas's imagination.

You can also help to develop your son's gifts by knowing when too much is too much. If you try to have too much control over his development, you may incite anger in him, or resentment. This will backfire on you. Don't make your expectations too high. Especially if your son is attempting to do something you were (or are) good at, give him room. Don't expect him to be even better. When your expectations are too high, it's impossible for your son to meet them. When I look at

Jesse's expectations for David, I almost want to laugh. While Jesse paraded his older boys in front of the prophet Samuel, he didn't even bother to bring in David from the fields. Jesse wasn't breathing down David's neck, expecting him to make something of himself.

Most importantly, you can show your son what you really believe about him by living it. Know who he is and what he's good at, don't be too hard on him, and affirm him by living out that you believe in him. Share with him how others have given you comfort and where God has given you the opportunity to comfort others. Let him see firsthand how a man uses what he has to bring comfort to others. Teach him not to shy away from giving comfort. Sometimes we think that a person will become dependent or weak if offered comfort. But comfort doesn't weaken people; it makes them stronger.

Comfort Brings Strength

Comfort is an interesting word. Do you see the word "fort" in it? A fort is a big place that offers shelter. It's strong; it protects. Boys love to play in forts, whether under blankets in a bedroom, in the woods or behind walls of snow. An army builds a fort. Frontiersmen built forts. The United States government stores gold in a fort. A fort is tough.

The word "comfort" is derived from *fortis*, the same Latin word that gives us the word "fort." Add the prefix "com" and you have a word that means, literally, to "give strength" (Merriam-Webster). Stop for a minute and think about the power of that idea. If someone is burdened and you comfort that person, you've given them strength. They don't feel as weak anymore. Or as despondent. Comfort also brings hope, and that strengthens a person. Someone can lose heart to the point that they may want to give up on life. Hope gives them strength to look past the present into the future.

The Bible gives many examples of God providing comfort to his people. There is even an example, in the book of Zechariah, of God comforting an angel. Our God knows how to comfort His people, and we learn from His example how to comfort others. Paul wrote his friends in Corinth about his experience with this. "God comforts us in all our troubles so that we can comfort those in any trouble," he explained (II Cor 1:4, NIV). As Eugene Peterson translates this passage: "He comes alongside us when we go through hard times, and before you know it, he brings us alongside someone else who is going through hard times so that we can be there for that person just as God was there for us" (The Message).

Daddy, teach your son how to come alongside of those going through hard times and to share comfort. Just as David learned to play a harp while growing up in the House of Jesse, let your son learn who he is and how he can become a man of talent while growing up in your care. David wasn't afraid to use his gift before a powerful, tormented king, so encourage your son to have the confidence to use his skill in whatever situation God places him. Let him see by your example that talents are entrusted to us for God's glory. When we comfort others, we glorify our Father in heaven.

Chapter 4

....

Fathers, Give Your Sons Solid Instruction
And Equip Them Properly

"So David got up early in the morning . . . and set out as Jesse had instructed him." I Samuel 17:20, HCS

Jesse wanted David to check on his three oldest brothers who were stationed at a military encampment under Saul's general. Jesse gave him detailed instructions about their geographic location and the army they were up against. "Check on the welfare of your brothers and bring a confirmation from them," he told David (I Samuel 17:18, HCS). Jesse organized the provisions he wanted David to take them, as well as a generous gift for the field commander. The Bible says that David rose early in the morning, made arrangements for someone else to look after the sheep, then loaded up the food "and set out as Jesse had instructed him."

When I study David's circumstances and the decisions he faced in these early chapters, I see a young man who was properly equipped for life. I believe Jesse gave him solid instruction as he grew up. David's long life is described in detail in the Bible—half of the thirty-one chapters in I Samuel and all twenty-four chapters in II Samuel are about David. But when he is first introduced, as a youth in I Samuel 16-18, I see clear evidence of his father's influence. These are David's earliest years, and the ones closest tied to the House of Jesse. Consider these clues of a father's solid instruction:

- David followed his dad's instructions to check on his brothers, taking a gift to the field commander. (I Samuel 17:18)
- David knew how to fight. (I Samuel 17:34-36)
- David also knew how to stay out of a fight. (I Samuel 17: 29)
- David showed respect to those in authority, referring to himself as a servant. (I Samuel 17:32)
- David wasn't afraid to speak up in the presence of powerful men. (I Samuel 17:39)

- Despite his achievements, David did not think too highly of himself. (I Samuel 18:23)
- When David went to work for Saul, his dad gave him a gift for the king. (I Samuel 16:20)
- Living in a strange place, David chose a friend with excellent character. (I Samuel 18:1)

David was properly equipped for both the people and the situations he encountered. In I Samuel 16 we read of how David went from a farm job to become the king's personal musician. Under pressure to perform for a difficult man, he remained calm and level headed, playing with skill in stressful circumstances. When my sons leave me, when they move out of my house, I want them to be properly equipped for life's challenges. I want them to know how to handle themselves in new situations. What is appropriate? What isn't? I want to teach them how to remain calm under pressure.

As I have thought about preparing my sons for the future, I have considered my role as their leader. I have looked around at other leaders to learn how they have instructed the people under them. That's why I decided to start giving a State of the Union address.

A Presidential Prerogative

As I listened to President Bush deliver his State of the Union address last year, I began to wonder what would happen if I gave a State of the Union address to my family. How would it be received? In fact, *what is the state of our union?*

It is the President's prerogative to evaluate the past year and look ahead to the future. He reviews significant events and lays out his plan for the next year. He alone can give the State of the Union address. He's the President. His vision properly equips the nation for what lies ahead.

I thought I'd give it a try.

I put on a suit and stood in front of the fireplace to deliver my first address in 2005. After some laughter, my wife and children listened quietly. Just as we listened closely to the President to learn his perspective, I discovered that my family wanted to hear mine.

This year, when I gave my second address, it was even more fun. Because I took notes during the year, I was well prepared. I spoke on four topics: the unity of our family, our faith, our finances, and our involvement in sports—which is an important issue for us. I graded us in each area.

Because our unity affects the climate in our house, I approached it by asking the question: Are we cheering each other on? Where I saw improvements I gave praise, where I saw gaps I made suggestions. Some members of the family have to work harder to understand the others. For example, my 13-year-old daughter Karsynn has a bent towards fashion and design, but her mother's interest is in the kitchen. "Karsynn," I said, "in order for you and your mom to grow closer, why don't you give in around the kitchen a little bit? And Loretta, sometimes you might go shopping—not to buy, but to look, for the design."

I reviewed our obedience and involvement at church. Were we taking faith-inspired risks? I also reviewed our track record in tithing, giving, saving and wasting money. I knew where we stood with the first three, but was unsure about the last. I told them I was leaving a question mark beside that one. I will study it more closely this year.

Finally, I talked to them about sports, not only about our involvement as a family, but also about our attitudes. Were we excited? Did we work at getting better? I evaluated how sports are impacting us as a family. Then came the report cards.

Shock and Awe

To my kids' amazement, I then presented each one with a personal report card. Some grades stung, some brought outbursts of laughter. On a few occasions, my wife and six kids were rolling. When I delivered a bad grade, there was the shock of disappointment, but for some of the A's, there was awe. I think my family appreciated the fact that Dad has been paying attention; I know them. I graded the children in five areas: their manners, appearance, obedience, faith, and friends.

You're probably not surprised that I would share with them my thoughts on their obedience, faith or friends. Did they readily obey what I asked? Have they grown in their faith from last year? And if so, in what ways? And are they choosing friends who have vision? Who encourage them to live up, not down?

But you may be surprised that I would grade them on their manners and appearance. In a culture where teenagers routinely say "whatever" when asked a question by an adult, parents face tremendous social pressure to compromise when teaching their children good manners and to dress appropriately. I am amazed at the way some of the young ladies dress these days. And young men are not being instructed on how to properly treat a lady.

It's not the first time there has been a setback in manners. William Wilberforce, who worked to get rid of the slave trade in England during the late 1700s, was overwhelmed by the bad manners of his day. On October 28, 1787, he wrote in his diary: "God Almighty has set before me two great objects, the suppression of the Slave Trade and the Reformation of Manners" (*Wilberforce*, John Pollock, Lion Publishing, 1977, page 69). Wilberforce was a key player in changing both. On July 26, 1833, when he was on his deathbed, the Abolition of Slavery Bill made it through its third reading in the House of Commons, an achievement that took fifty years of unthinkable setbacks and discouragements. This great Christian man dedicated his life to improving the way people, as a society, treated each other. Enslaving human beings and bad manners have this in common: both scoff at treating others with respect.

Loretta and I are intentionally teaching our children, especially our sons, the value of good manners. For their report cards I graded their manners at home and in public. I also graded their appearance—their efforts to be clean and well groomed—at social events, church and school. We don't want doors to close on our children because of their ignorance. Recently, when Korde met privately with President Bush, we were glad we had taught him a proper handshake. We have equipped him to be a future president of the United States.

Hail to the Chief

That's right. No, we don't have some crazy idea that all of our children are going to the White House or Hollywood, but we do have the idea that wherever they go, they should feel comfortable. We don't want poor instruction on our part to prevent them from receiving God's best for them. One day we hope they will thank us. For example, we have taught our sons to not reach out to shake a lady's hand unless she extends hers first. We've taught them proper etiquette at the table. In a culture that can't seem to bring the cell phone under control, where instant satisfaction is expected—if not demanded—we have the opportunity to show our children a better way, the way of waiting. They can *wait* to speak on the cell phone after they've gone through a checkout line. I've seen so many cashiers look downcast as people complete a transaction without so much as acknowledging their presence. Our kids can *wait* to begin eating after the hostess has lifted her fork. They can *wait* their turn to play with a new toy that's exciting. They can *wait* to speak without interrupting the person who is talking. Little waits lead to bigger waits, such as *waiting* for the right spouse or *waiting* for God to provide financially. Teaching them to wait on God, to take the route that God designs, begins with us. As we struggle to stay on the right path, we can share with them what God is teaching us. This gives them a living example to follow.

I well remember looking desperately for an example to follow when I flew to New York to be on the Good Morning America show in 1982. There was so much protocol in that fast-paced world, and I felt unprepared. I hate not knowing what to do. While there, Coach Danny Ford and I attended a black tie dinner at the Waldorf Astoria. I remember studying the other men at the table to figure out what was proper. Fathers, we don't want our sons looking around for somebody to show them what to do. We want them to become men who lead, not follow. Let's give them the confidence to be decisive in whatever situation God has them. By giving our sons proper instruction, even on things as simple as how to go to lunch with the boss, we sweep away a lot of the noise that the world uses to distract them. We want them to hear the still, small voice of God.

It's like learning to concentrate on the game when 80,000 people are screaming all around you. How can we teach our sons to run out onto that field and play? Despite all of the noise, the excitement, and the distractions, they have the opportunity to participate with the God of the Universe in the game He is in. There is a lot of noise up in the stands, but the playing is on the field. We want our boys on the field, concentrating on the game, learning from the Coach. We want them to follow us into Death Valley.

Our Sons Learn by Running With Us

I was getting too old for this. My bad knees were scaring me, and I had a downhill run just ahead. I would be leading the Clemson football team into Death Valley, the nickname for the university's football stadium. Begun in the 1940s, the stadium was built in a valley on the west side of campus. The name came from Coach Lonnie McMillan of Presbyterian College whose team kept getting whipped every time they played there. He started calling it Death Valley. The stadium is one of the ten largest college football stadiums in the country and regularly has crowds of 80,000, most of them dressed in orange. When Georgia lost to us in 1981, Herschel Walker said the noise was so bad he had trouble concentrating. Former Duke quarterback Dave Brown said he was so intimidated by the Death Valley reputation, and the thought of 80,000 people dressed in orange, that he threw up before the game—the only time he's ever done that. When the Clemson team runs down the hill into the stadium, it's incredible. Brent Musberger of ABC Sports has called it "the most exciting 25 seconds in college football."

This was the Florida State game of 2002 and I had been asked to lead the team in. That morning, as I was driving to Clemson, my oldest son Korde was riding with me. I prayed silently as I drove about a burden I was carrying: "Lord, how can I get Korde to understand that life with You means he is participating with the *God of the Universe*?" I longed for Korde to grasp the incredible excitement of the Christian life—that we participate with God in His work here on Earth. Jesus said, "it is the Father, living in me, who is doing his work" (John 14:10, NIV). God has the same plan for us, Christ living in us, doing His work. For some time I had praying that God would help me explain this to Korde.

Now I was at the top of the hill. The 3:30 game was going to be broadcast across the nation by ABC Sports. I was getting ready to do something I had never done before: I was taking my son with me. A few hours earlier I had asked Korde, "Son, what would make your day today?" Immediately he had answered, "Dad, if I could run down the hill with you!" I dismissed it instantly. "Korde, you can't do that. That's only for players." But then I began to ask myself the question, If Korde doesn't run down the hill with me, who will he run down with? If I'm not taking him into the arena of life to face the crowds, who will? So I made arrangements for him to run with the team. With cameras in our faces, the cannon went off and we started running—I was hoping my knees would stay intact. People were going crazy; my son got lost in the crowd. As the game started I found him and we stood on the sidelines. I had an idea.

"Korde, listen," I said. "I want you to close your eyes. When I tell you to open them, I want you to look at the upper deck. Don't look at the field or the lower deck—just open your eyes and tell me what you see." My 12-year-old son opened his eyes and stared up into the crowds in the high decks over the valley. The roar was deafening. "Dad," he hesitated, "I see, I see . . . spectators. I see fans. I see orange everywhere."

"Now close your eyes again," I said. "This time, don't look at the spectators, don't look at the crowd. I want you to look at the field and tell me what you see."

Again he opened his eyes. "Dad, I see players. I see football players." He looked at me with a question on his face, wondering where I was going with all of this. I began to point out the players.

"See that number 68 for Florida State?" I asked him. "He's a pulling guard. He's going to lead the running back around the end. He's going to lead the way; he's a blocker. See that defensive back? He only weighs about 175 pounds. That big offensive lineman weighs about 300 pounds." What a threat. Who wants to run into that kind of wall?

"Here's the thing, Korde, it takes courage to be a player. If it starts to rain today, guess what the spectator will do? He's going to go home. To be a player means you stay, even when it's raining. A player wants to participate. There's something he wants to win."

As I looked at how few men were on the field and at the tens of thousands in the stands, another thought occurred to me.

"Son, spectators usually come to a game in a crowd. Players, they don't mind playing by themselves, even in the backyard." I looked at Korde for a second then I asked him, "Korde, do you want to be a spectator, or do you want to be a player?"

"Dad, I want to be a player."

A few minutes later, as we made our way up through the stands to the president's box, I told him, "Korde, on the way home, I'm going to tell you how to be a player." I said this by faith because I didn't have a plan. But I trusted that God would provide and show me how to use this.

Hours later, we were in the car headed home and he asked me, "Dad, what was that all about—that player/spectator thing? What was that all about?"

All of a sudden, God spoke to my heart.

"Korde, tomorrow we are going to go to church. There are going to be thousands upon thousands of men sitting in pews all over our city. There will be hundreds in our church. And Korde, they are only spectators. Don't get me wrong—they are going to go to heaven—they are part of the team. But they don't want to play because they don't want to be injured. They don't want to see a 300-pounder coming after them. They don't have courage. They come in a crowd, and they stay in the crowd. They just want to blend in. Very few people want to be players in God's kingdom.

"Korde, I want to challenge you to ask God that if he's looking for a starting quarterback, in His game, that he would choose you."

Dads, I could not have come up with that on my own. In prayer, God helped me to say what my son needed to hear. God took a moment in my son's life and spoke to him through a picture he could understand.

When I pray, I'm looking for God around the corners of my life. I want to see some things I've never seen before and I want to pass those things on. Unlike other aspects of the Christian life, prayer is the only thing that truly belongs to me. If I want to do something in the church building, I have to ask permission. If I give money, a group of elders decides where it goes. But what I do in prayer is mine. I can do it whenever I want, wherever I want—it belongs to me. Because it belongs to me, it's the one thing that gets me close to God.

Through prayer we find our children's teachable moments. The normal, everyday things we do with our families as well as the special things provide opportunities for solid instruction. We look for what God is doing and get in His game. Jesus said, "the Son can do nothing by himself; he can do only what he sees his Father doing, because whatever the Father does the Son also does" (John 5:19, NIV). What do you see the Father doing in your son's life? Find out what He is doing and join Him. Jesus also said, "anyone who has faith in me will do what I have been doing" (John 14:12, NIV). Look for what He is doing and have faith to join Him.

The House of Jesse is a House of Learning

What you know and share with your son will equip him for life. He will learn things from you that he will never learn from another man. You, alone, have the time, the opportunity, and the position to teach him what he needs to know. You can teach him about girls, you can teach him about football. You can teach him about prayer, you can teach him how to act on a date. You can teach him to wait, you can teach him to lead. Your house is a house of learning.

Trust God to lead you as you pray, and be willing to step out in faith. Even if you don't know where something is going, follow Him. He will surprise you. The life of faith in Christ is an adventure—let your son see that it's the best adventure you've ever experienced. Bring him alongside of you, into God's game.

Chapter 5

••••••••••••••••••••••

Fathers, Show Your Sons That
A True Champion Is A Man Of Faith

"The Philistine champion, Goliath of Gath, stepped out from the front lines of the Philistines, and gave his usual challenge. David heard him. . . . 'I'm about to kill you, cut off your head, and serve up your body and the bodies of your Philistine buddies to the crows and coyotes . . . . everyone gathered here will learn that GOD doesn't save by means of sword or spear.'"
I Samuel 17:23, 46-47, The Message

Goliath was a champion in his country. Towering above other men, his size alone intimidated those who saw him. "When the Israelites saw the man, they all ran from him in great fear" (I Samuel 17: 24, NIV). He stood over nine feet tall—the ceiling height in many of today's upscale homes. His armor weighed as much as a lot of men's wives, 126 pounds. That didn't include his shin guards, which were made of bronze. His sword was also of bronze and the spear he carried had a tip that weighed fifteen pounds.

He had mass. He had density. He had volume.

He was a known killer. King Saul told David, "he has been a fighting man from his youth" (verse 33, NIV). He was a celebrated champion on the field of battle. He knew how to kill. He knew the smell of blood, the last suck of breath when he pulled out his sword. He was so good at it that the entire Philistine army chose him as their representative. They knew he could kill anyone he went up against.

As a champion, Goliath understood how to taunt the opposition. A good fight is not just about the knock out, it's about breaking your opponent's will. No armor can protect a man against fear, and Goliath instinctively knew how to break the enemy's will through fear. He dressed the part, and then he followed up with psychological warfare. Read closely his words of challenge. He had the ego and bravado of a man who knew he was going to beat anyone who crossed him. Walking out onto the battlefield in plain view of every soldier, he shouted for a fight.

His strategy worked. By playing the offense, he put the entire Israeli army on the defense. They were scared. A true champion has already visualized beating his enemy before the fight begins. Goliath knew how to start that fight and finish it. He made the first move. He was poised for victory.

David, however, had tasted a power that Goliath knew nothing of. David knew the adrenaline of faith. Goliath had unwittingly crossed a line that David knew was a fatal error: He was mocking the living God and defying His army. David's faith-walk with God brought him to a place of absolute confidence against such threats. His friendship with God made him a champion unlike any Goliath had encountered. He had a weapon Goliath had never used: faith.

How the World Defines a Champion

In David's time, a champion was a military hero. The Bible introduces Goliath as "the Philistine champion." When he fought, he won. The world declared him a champion by one standard: winning.

In many ways, professional sports have become a modern day substitute for the battlefield. We live in a world that makes heroes and champions out of sports superstars. We can't drive our SUV to a Kansas field and watch American soldiers whip foreign troops. But that desire to fight is still within a man, and we need a champion. When sports heroes lead their teams to victory, we cheer them on as they outsmart, outmaneuver, and out muscle the losing teams. When they win, they are our champions. If they lose, we analyze their failures. The fight that is inside of us gets transferred to them.

Like the rest of the world, we define a champion by winning.

But where does that leave us when our champions let us down? And what do we do with their moral failures? We're ambivalent. In June 2003, an NBA player was accused of sexual assault at a Colorado hotel. Although the case was settled out of court, the accusations left a bad taste with many fans. How long did that last? In February of this year, Kobe Bryant began appearing in Nike ads to promote the Zoom Kobe I sneaker. In the ad he says this about himself: "A champion. Hate that. Hate it with all your heart. And hate that I'm loved, for the exact same reasons." Flaunting his controversial reputation, Bryant calls himself a champion, confident of his claim. A champion is a winner, and he knows *he is a winner*.

I spend a lot of time with pro-athletes and serve as chaplain for an NBA team. Many of these young men struggle to handle the fame, power, and money thrown at them. Their talents have put them in the limelight. Not their character.

A Champion From the House of Jesse

David had a big fight inside of him, and it was the fight to honor God. Later in his life, he would take up fights that he should have avoided. But as a young man, emerging from the House of Jesse, he was a champion who rose to defend the honor of his God. As David explained to Saul, "he [Goliath] has defied the armies of the living God. The Lord who delivered me from the paw of the lion and the paw of the bear will deliver me from the hand of this Philistine" (I Samuel 17:36-37).

This was a man after God's heart. For centuries afterwards, David stood out in Jewish history as a champion driven by an inner sense of right and wrong. He was the kind of champion captured in such contemporary movies as *Gladiator* and *Braveheart*. Heroes like Maximus and William Wallace possess a moral courage that cannot be defeated by military superiority. They fight for something greater than their own power. For David, that something greater was God. The apostle Paul spoke of David's legendary reputation on his first missionary journey, over a thousand years after David's birth. During a sermon at the synagogue in Antioch, he quoted what God told the prophet Samuel: "I have found David the son of Jesse, a man after My heart, who will carry out all My will" (Acts 13:22, HCS). David was a champion who understood what was on God's mind and in His heart. He foreshadowed the real champion God would one day send into the world.

Training to Fight for Lasting Rewards

Most of the world is looking for a champion who will take care of the obvious. In Jesus' day, the Jews wanted someone to beat the Romans. In his 2005 biography, the rock star Bono imagined Christ saying something along these lines: "I know you're expecting me to come back with an army, and set you free from these creeps, but actually I am the Messiah" (*Bono: In Conversation with Michka Assayas*, Penguin). Christ had a fight to win that was bigger than the Romans. As dads, we think if we teach our sons to take care of the obvious, we've done our job. I know many fathers who have taught their sons important lessons about money and advancing their careers. These things are significant, but they don't produce a true champion. At the end of the day, do their boys know how to pray? How to read God's word? How to treat a woman? Have they learned that a true champion is a man of faith as well as of action?

The Fights We Choose

Our sons are watching us and taking notes on the fights we choose. Let's ask ourselves the question: Are the fights we're choosing God's fights? Are we about our Father's business? Or are we picking up where our earthly fathers left off?

I'll never forget the first time my wife, Loretta, met my dad. He had blood all over him. He had been in a fistfight. He was drunk. Here I was, playing with the Atlanta Falcons, introducing my future bride to my dad, and he had just been in a fight. I wished I had seen my dad fight for civil rights. Or fight for the reading of scripture and its proper interpretation. Or fight for his marriage, showing through tough times and hard times that a marriage is not easy, but it is worth fighting for. Like other sons before me, I have fallen into fighting the fights that were important to my father. It's the default position. For many black men, those fights are race fights. Even if we're not chasing them, they chase us. Like the one that cornered me in a car one day.

Loretta and I were at a stop light near a large mall, the windows down and the sunroof open. It was a good day because Loretta was driving. I was taking in the warm air. Looking to my right, I noticed a nice looking car with two guys — white men. They were sharp looking, dressed up. Since they were looking at me, I nodded, expecting a friendly gesture back. One called to me, "Hey niggers, go home!"

That got my attention. "What did you say?" I asked, my blood rising. "Niggers, go home!" they repeated. I grabbed the steering wheel from Loretta's grasp (we were turning left, they were going straight) and Loretta grabbed me. "Perry, what are you doing?" she said. I began to get angry with her. "Get out of the car and let me drive," I demanded. Here I was, a Christian and an elder in the church. She would not let me get behind the wheel. I wanted to fight.

This literally spoiled my day. Back home, I wasn't sure if I was madder at the men or Loretta. I retreated into my study, silent. Some time passed, then Loretta appeared in the doorway, coming with her wisdom. "Perry, can I say something to you?" she asked. I did not say anything, so she continued. "Perry, I know there are some people who want to communicate with you. They're all outside in the backyard waiting for you to play. Then there are two other people, somewhere in this city, who are probably not even thinking about you right now, but you are spending all of your time thinking about them." Then she turned and walked away.

It's hard on me when Loretta is right. The truth was, I had picked up a fight that my dad passed on to me because he hated white people. I started fighting the fight that meant a lot to him. We have a generation of fathers who are not picking their own fights. We need to figure out the fights Jesus chose and join him.

The Champion's Life

"Do you take Katherine to be your lawful wedded wife, to love, honor, comfort and cherish her from this day forward?" My son was squirming. I was asking him if he could see himself saying these words to the young girl he wanted to date. To his embarrassment, I was walking him through a traditional wedding vow. Like most teenage boys, the thought of marriage had not entered his mind. In fact, most of the men I know don't look at these words until they're on their way to the altar.

For most of our sons, God will give them a woman to love. He gave a bride to Adam and He also gave a bride to Christ. From the first Adam to the last Adam we see God's desire that a husband know how to love his wife. I see three key areas in which we can challenge our sons to live as champions like David, to live as men of faith. The first mark of that life is obedience. Will they learn God's will and then obey Him? David wrote, "I delight to do your will, O my God" (Psalm 40:8, NAS). God has a will; David learned what it was and obeyed it. Even as a young man he demonstrated a willingness to be obedient to Jesse, traveling back and forth between Saul's camp and home, leaving a fight to take care of sheep. He was obedient to his father, and later, to Saul, even though Saul's purposes towards him were twisted. But David's faith was not in Saul, it was in his God.

Secondly, God has a work for our sons to do. He places a calling on each man's life. Although the specifics may not become clear until our boys are in their twenties or thirties, they have a unique work appointed by God. "For we are God's workmanship, created in Christ Jesus to do good works, which God prepared in advance for us to do" (Ephesians 2:10, NIV). We want to encourage them to wait on God and to embrace their calling. If they become dependent on their feelings, it will be hard to have the discipline to follow God's calling. Jesus set the example for us by living above his feelings. In the most basic example, he resisted his feelings of hunger and the opportunity to satisfy himself when tempted in the desert by the Devil. This obedience prepared Him for the work God had for him to do. As our sons face the ordinary issues of life, and respond with obedience, God prepares them for the work ahead.

Let me make a comment here about obedience. It is not simply an act of the will. It is an act of faith. We do not want to give our sons the impression that they can whip up the power to obey God, as though sheer determination can see them through. No, that's what a Pharisee thinks. Jesus called people who thought like this hypocrites: "Woe to you, scribes and Pharisees, hypocrites! You pay a tenth of mint, dill, and cumin, yet you have neglected the more important matters of the law—justice, mercy, and faith." (Matthew 23:23 HCS). "Faith" is one of "the more important matters of the law." We have to be born again to live a life of obedience because to really obey God requires faith. It took faith for Noah to build a boat that would survive catastrophic rainstorms, especially since he had never seen rain. God told him what to do, but he had to believe before he could obey. As Paul says, "obedience comes from faith" (Romans 1:5 NIV). So in order for our sons to live an obedient life and to embrace the work God has for them, they need faith.

The third key area of the champion life is how they love their bride. We must call our sons to live like champions in all three areas, to live a life marked by faith in God's plans and purposes. But we must first understand those plans and purposes in order to explain them to our boys.

The Shadow

In the story of Peter Pan, his shadow seems to have a life of its own. When the nursery window is slammed shut, Peter's shadow is snapped off. After being captured, it is rolled up and stored in a drawer. When Peter comes back for it, it won't stay on and Wendy has to sew it to his feet. Although it has no face and is made of darkness, Peter's shadow scampers about, mischievous and unruly.

A shadow is the likeness of the one who casts it. Shadows are made by the absence of light and we usually think of them negatively. A son may "live in his father's shadow," meaning he can't seem to carve out an identity of his own. An evil empire may "cast a shadow" across a time or place, so that its influence is felt beyond its borders. A robber may "stand in the shadows" or "hide in the shadows." David wrote about walking through the valley of "the shadow of death" (Psalm 23:4) and described man's days on earth "like a fleeting shadow" (Psalm 144:4). A business deal that does not seem to be on the up-and-up is said to be "shady," or made in the shadows.

We are descended from the first Adam and naturally live in the dark image of his shadow. If we make no effort to do otherwise, we will act like him in our marriages. Our sons, also, will follow his example. As men, we all live in our father's shadow. This daddy, Adam, casts a shadow across us that draws us into silence and passivity. It is an influence that feminizes young men. If we do not learn from the second Adam—Christ—how a man is to treat his bride, then we will live in this "shadow of death."

That is not the life of a champion.

Most men are still living in the shadow of the first Adam. What do I mean by that? They are passive around their wives. They may provide, but they don't protect. They may listen, but they don't lead. They are quiet when they should be speaking words of faith. They protect themselves while exposing the woman.

When I read the account of what happened in the Garden of Eden, I imagine that Adam was standing close by when the serpent spoke to Eve. Perhaps he was hanging back, standing in the shadows, waiting to see what would happen if Eve took fruit from the forbidden tree and ate it. Would she die? What would that look like? He exposed her to danger and did not stop what was happening. We have no record of Adam objecting to what she was doing, or contradicting the serpent's claims. The Bible only tells us that he "was with her, and he ate it" (Genesis 3:6, NIV).

He was with her.

He listened to her, too, and didn't contradict her. A man who had the intuition and confidence to boldly name all of the animals simply listened when his wife talked to him about the sin she was thinking of committing. God later judged him for this failure. It wasn't just that he ate of the fruit, but it was "because you *listened to your wife* and ate" (Genesis 3:17). How many of us know when our wife is veering into a danger zone, but we stay quiet and simply listen? We're not deceived, we're passive. We decide to sit down and watch the game instead of getting involved in a conversation that we don't feel like having. In Eve's defense, at least we know that she was clearly deceived. She admits it (Genesis 3:13), a fact Paul later points out in a letter to Timothy (I Timothy 2:14). But Adam was not deceived, which Paul also notes. Men, for many of us the problem is not that we are deceived; the problem is that we don't want to act. We want to wait and see what happens.

How is it that a man can be decisive, clear, energetic, and a leader in the marketplace, but then come home and step into the shadows?

But let us see how a true champion acts.

Another man in the Bible was given a bride. When she was lost, He searched for her. When she did not know the direction to take, He said, "follow me." When she did things that showed her ignorance, He taught her. When she was tempted, He promised her, "I will not let you be tempted beyond what you can bear" (I Corinthians 10:13). When she needed to talk, He listened. When she was going to die, He took her place. He willingly gave His life as a ransom for hers.

Do you know why I think Jesus was born of a virgin? I believe it was because God did not want his son to have the DNA of the first Adam. He wanted a real man, a man not infected with guessing, a man not marked by passivity.

This is our champion. He sets the example.

Fight For the Trophy

Daddy, it's easy to get discouraged when you see the challenge. Our enemy is strong. But our God is bigger and He promises to reward us if we will fight for the trophy. Your sons are worth the fight. As an Old Testament prophet told a king who faced a hard task, "be strong and do not give up, for your work will be rewarded" (II Chronicles 15:7). We can live as champions through the power Christ gives us.

God has promised to give us the victory (I Corinthians 15:57). All we need to do is to "run in such a way as to get the prize" (I Corinthians 9:24). What is the way that we should run? It is the way of faith. As John explained, "This is the victory that has overcome the world, even our faith" (I John 5:4, NIV). There is power in believing God. Remember that David was the kind of champion God honored: he was a man of faith. The result? "The Lord gave David victory everywhere he went" (I Chronicles 18:13).

Never forget that God is a rewarder of those who seek Him (Hebrews 11:6). Without faith it is impossible to please Him; with it, nothing is impossible.

Chapter 6

....

Fathers, Give Your Sons
A Reason To Come Home

My brother Eddie

First year of high school

My grandfather Robert Melton
(He lived to be 100 years old.)

My dad Russell "Sam" Tuttle with my mom

My dad and me

Freshman as a Tiger

My rookie year with the Buffalo Bills

Wide Receiver for the Atlanta Falcons

Freshman year at Clemson

My mother Betty Tuttle and high school coach Pete Jones when I signed to attend Clemson University

Jeff Davis (my roommate for 4 years) and me
with a live tiger

Perry Tuttle

Perry playing for CFL Winnipeg
Bluebombers

Perry Tuttle

Return kickoff in the Orange Bowl

Just Because You're Dad...

... You have a special warm embrace.
... You taught me about God's never-ending grace.
... You taught me how to play—basketball, football, bike riding, and how to pray.
... Thank you for the legacy you've given me.
... Forever grateful, I will be.

Your First Born Son,

Korde Kensington Tuttle

My favorite drawing from my little boy Korde

Perry and wife Loretta

My dad Sam and mom Betty with brother Eddie

Perry with Loretta and their children: Korde, Karsynn, Karigan, Kanyon, Kallaway and Kambridge

"David went back and forth from Saul to tend his father's sheep at Bethlehem." I Samuel 17: 14, NIV

David's brothers enlisted in the army, so he traveled between his father's house and the army encampment to check on them. After seeing how they were, he would head back home, no doubt bringing comfort to his aging father whom the Bible describes as "old and well advanced in years. As the youngest of eight sons, David had a practical reason to come home—he was in charge of the sheep.

David was eventually pulled away from these duties by a higher authority. When he killed Goliath, Saul brought him to live at his house. There was no more going "back and forth" to take care of his father's sheep at Bethlehem. Rather, "from that day Saul kept David with him and did not let him return to his father's house" (I Samuel 18:1).

Saul would not let David go back home. If keeping up with his chores was the only reason David had to go home, perhaps he and his dad would have drifted apart. Maybe that would be the end of the House of Jesse. But David had closer ties to his father than that. We read a small but significant mention of their relationship several chapters later.

After Saul revealed his plan to murder David, David escaped with the help of Saul's son, Jonathan. He ended up hiding out in a cave. When his brothers and parents heard about this, they went to him. This could not have been a safe situation for an elderly father, either politically or physically. Out of concern for his parents' safety, David decided to pay a visit to the king of Moab. "Would you let my father and mother come and stay with you until I learn what God will do for me?" he asked (I Samuel 22: 3). The king agreed, and David left his parents with him.

A Heart for Home
David's heart was invested in his home, even when he

left to assume responsibilities in other places. When he went to check on his brothers in the army, he never failed to come back home and pick up where he left off. When he was commanded by the country's top leader to relocate, David moved. But he didn't forget about home. Even as an outlaw, David stayed in touch with his parents and was concerned about their welfare.

I ask myself, what took place in the House of Jesse that created such a strong bond? What reason did Jesse give his son for coming home? David saw the exciting life his brothers were living, the life of soldiers—the danger, the friendship, the fights and challenges—yet he continued to return home to his dad. We know that David had the heart of a warrior because he became Israel's greatest military hero, yet he also had the heart of a son. He had a reason to return home that was stronger than his personality or talents.

We should ask ourselves, what reason will I give my own sons to come home? As we look at the House of Jesse, "home" is not just a place, it's a relationship. A father has a strong influence over a son's desire to be at home. If he cares about his boy, and is faithful to be at home himself, his son will want to be with him. Society falls apart when a father's heart is not turned towards his children, when the home becomes a place of failure, not success. When the home is empty, the heart follows. I find it interesting that the Old Testament ends with a promise to shake up the family. The last verse of Malachi states that God will "turn the hearts of the fathers to their children, and the hearts of the children to their fathers" (Malachi 4:6). This is the last thing we read before the Messiah is announced in Matthew 1.

In a Cave Without Dad

Our church has a ministry to prisons that reaches across two states. Every month or so, I have the opportunity to travel to a prison and speak to the inmates. Sometimes I speak in a chapel; once I spoke to over a hundred-and-fifty men crowded into a shock unit of a South Carolina prison. It was a big, cement-floored room with bunk beds lining the walls. It was so hot that I was sweating in my short sleeves, even though it was January. Two female wardens shouted orders at the inmates—angry women controlling angry men. It was depressing.

At another prison, closer to home, I had an experience far more troubling. As I was preparing to speak, a man walked close to me and spoke my name. I turned to see the brother of a friend who was in my wedding. "Brad?" I said, alarmed. His family lived right down the street from where I grew up. "What are you doing here?" I asked him, hardly believing my eyes. Immediately I thought about his dad. Brad's father lived in the home, in the same house, but he never *showed up*. "Now here's Brad, stuck in this place," I thought, sickened.

There are so many talented young men, especially young black boys, who are headed in this direction. According to recent statistics from the U.S. Department of Justice, it is estimated that about one third of black men will enter state or federal prison during their lifetime. *One third*. Let that sink in. Don't think about a drug dealer wearing gold chains. Think about a six-year-old boy you saw recently at the mall, a boy who doesn't have a dad in his life. He's the one we should be thinking about when we hear this statistic. In 2002, Dr. Wade F. Horn, the Assistant Secretary for Children and Families of the U.S. Department of Health and Human Services, said, "The most consequential social trend of our time is the dramatic increase in the number of children growing up in father-absent families."

A father-absent family opens the door for everyone else to leave. And by the way, you don't have to be a black man in prison to be absent from your home. A highly paid CEO can come home from work at night and check out. A phone call, a ball game, a meeting . . . there are plenty of places for us to stand in the shadows with Adam. What is the answer? It's not staring at the problem, it's looking at the solution. We need a vision of what "home" should look like to a boy. We need to give our sons a reason to come home.

"No Contact, No Impact"

That's a favorite saying of my close friend Steve Jirgal, a pastor who has two sons and a daughter. I've been meeting with Steve just about every Friday for the last fourteen years — he's been my mentor since Loretta graded me, at my request, on being a husband. That night in the restaurant was a turning point in my life. With tears streaming down her gentle face, Loretta honestly answered my questions about how I was doing as a friend, husband and father. Wow, the things you aren't prepared to hear. Especially in a public place where others are watching. After that, I realized I needed help. Steve has been faithfully meeting with me throughout these years and has become my close friend.

When their oldest son became a teenager, and a second son was not far behind, Steve and his wife, Pam, began to take a hard look at their house. How could they give their boys a reason to come home? They wanted to make an environment that would be a magnet for teenage kids. They didn't like the idea of unsupervised teenagers hanging out in neighborhood houses after school, a temptation that would increase as their boys got older — their neighborhood is swamped with middle school and high school boys. "We know what our kids are doing here, at home, because they're with us," Steve says. "But we don't always know what they're doing at the neighbors'."

Above Steve's woodworking shop was an empty room that was used for drying wood. He and Pam decided that would have to go. Working slowly, one project at a time, they began to turn the room into a place kids would love. Steve stayed focused on what he hoped his kids would one day say to their friends: "Come home with me — we always have a great time there!" On a pastor's modest salary, and doing most of the work himself, Steve transformed this room. When he and Pam finished putting in the air conditioning last summer, they had built a teenage boy's dream getaway. The room has a pool table, an air hockey table, a sitting area to play games, and an entertainment center with all of the Play Station II equipment.

Underneath the ping pong table's removable top is a train track with Lionel trains. There's even a drink machine. "With that many kids, we'd go broke buying drinks," Steve says, laughing. So kids can buy a soda for a quarter.

"Our goal is to keep our kids at home," Steve says. What wise parents they are. Rather than investing in an expensive car or some other temporary pleasure, Steve and Pam are investing in a mission. They know these years will be short, and they are staying focused on their goal: to walk with their children through the culture they live in, showing them how to be in this world but not of it.

By making contact, they are having an impact.

Finding a Strategy

Steve and Pam are giving their kids a great reason to come home: laughter, fun together, and a sense of belonging. They are demonstrating that home is a place you can bring others to, a place where the door is open. Friends are welcome. They are modeling hospitality, generosity, and honest enjoyment to their children and the neighborhood. Because they are spending time with the neighborhood kids, they're available when someone needs to talk. In turn, they also earn the right to ask the hard questions.

This is so different from my experience growing up. I was careful to go home only when I knew my father *wasn't* there. My home was an intimidating place. My dad let it be known that the top priority in his house was one person: himself. The fear factor was strong. I thank God that my father became my best friend in later years, and many of these painful memories lost their power. But if you're like me, you may feel somewhat at a loss to know how to establish a really good home. You probably understand the story I've shared about Steve—after all, who doesn't want to have fun at home? We can all start there. I'd like to offer a few more ideas.

Love What You Have

As awkward as it felt, I took Loretta's face in my hands and gently whispered, "I love you." I could feel several sets of little eyes staring up at this exchange, taking it all in. I was at home and I had decided to be more purposeful in showing affection. This is so tough for me — showing emotion to my wife, especially in front of the children. But I believe that my boys need to see their dad touch his wife, take her hand, or look in her face and tell her he loves her. When a husband shows his wife affection in the presence of the children, he sends a strong message. His commitment to his wife becomes real to them.

Daddy, when you are at home, love what you have. Love your wife. Help your children to see that a family is full of different kinds of people who, at the core, are committed to the same things. They love each in many different ways. "Observe how Christ loved us," Paul wrote. "Love like that" (Ephesians 5:2, The Message).

The other night I took four different kinds of apples and held them in my hands. I had a Red Delicious, a Golden Delicious, a Granny Smith, and a Jonagold. They looked different, from deep red to bright green to a mix of red and yellow. They also tasted different. I walked in to where the children were and, smiling, asked them, "What do I have in my hands?" They knew I was up to something, and the youngest, my two-year-old son who loves to play games, piped up: "They're apples!"

"Yes," I said, "all of them are called apples even though they all look different and they taste different." I gave them a chance to see the colors and shapes. Then I took a knife and split two of them.

"But at the core, they're all the same. They look the same." In the middle of each half was a dark core holding a cluster of shiny seeds. By this point, I had their attention. "We're all different in this family, but at the core of the Tuttles, of who we are as a family, there are some things that will always be the same," I explained, then I gave some examples. "The children in this family will always address older people with a title, such as coach or pastor or uncle," I said. Respect for others is at the core of being a Tuttle. "And we want to know God," I continued. "On the outside we all look different. If we look at Karsyn, she looks different from Korde. Yet we can say that at the core, these are the main ingredients. This is who we are."

The kids seemed delighted and pleased. One of my girls expressed relief. "So I'm not weird!" she said. As simple as this exercise was, it reinforced a message I wanted my children to understand: I respect who you are and I acknowledge that you are different. You have the freedom in this house to develop into the person God created you to be. I believe in you. And I also believe that at your core, you are still a Tuttle. You belong in this family.

I want my children to understand that *I love what I have.* I'm not wishing they were someone else. I don't want a crop of clones. We're noticeably different in how we look and the way we think, but I love that. And I love who they are.

Set Up the Screen Pass

In football, a successful screen pass fools the defense and opens a lane for the receiver to catch the ball and run.

Have you ever considered that your son needs a screen of blockers? Men who can protect him when he receives the pass to run into manhood? Your son needs a community of men around him—your friends—who will block for him. When you pass the ball, these men will step into harm's way to clear your son's path.

I mentioned Steve Jirgal earlier and Steve and I have talked a lot about the medieval concept of knights. Both of us have developed relationships with other fathers who see the need to shepherd their sons from adolescence into manhood. Robert Lewis's book, *Raising a Modern-Day Knight*, has inspired many of us to examine the knighthood model for bringing sons to maturity. During the Middle Ages, a young boy who was destined to become a knight started off as a page. From the ages of seven to thirteen, he learned to serve. The next phase was that of a squire. During these years, from thirteen to seventeen, he was an apprentice. Discipline and responsibility were important. He learned the manhood language and how a man behaved. At eighteen he became a knight. A ceremony marked his entrance into manhood.

Adopting a medieval ceremony can't rescue our sons from a natural bent toward self-centeredness. But this approach has given Steve and me, and many other men, a lot to think about regarding our roles as fathers. We have become more intentional in creating ceremonies for our sons. We have sought the companionship of other men. We have become screens for each other's sons. As our sons are growing up, they are witnessing a community of men who clearing the field for them to take the ball and run. We are looking out for their interests, not just ours. We are learning what it means to "care about them as much as you care about yourselves" (Philippians 2:4, CEV).

Go Deep

Another pass route we talk about in football is "going deep." Bob Hayes, the Olympic gold-medal sprinter and receiver for the Dallas Cowboys made this his aim. He set a world record for the hundred-yard dash in 1963 and was called the fastest man alive. The next year he won a Gold Medal for the relay and set another world record. Then he started playing football. He was so fast that opposing players couldn't keep up with him. Other teams had to develop a zone defense. Hayes stayed focused on going deep. As fathers, we can draw our sons home by becoming men who go deep. In our conversations with them and in our personal journey of faith, we can be a living example that life in Christ will take them straight into the heart of the game.

How do we go deep? By faith.

I really began to learn this lesson in 1992 when I paid

cash for a very nice, European car. Around this same time, Loretta's brother walked out of his marriage—drove out, actually—leaving a wife and two sons without a car. She couldn't get to work. As Loretta talked to her—her sister-in-law—she began to pray. Soon Loretta felt we needed to give our new car to Lucy. I thought she was crazy. I said, "We'll help her buy a car." We just got our car. It was two or three weeks old.

Loretta asked me to pray about it, but I ignored her. Finally, I agreed to pray. Strangely, I began to hear the same thing from God. We ended up giving this car, title and everything, to Lucy, a sister-in-law. Even her family thought that we were crazy.

Within a month, I was unexpectedly out of football, forced to retire. My nice car was gone and now I was driving an ugly, little minivan. I hate minivans. We moved back to South Carolina—my career was over.

In Clemson we stopped by a car dealership to say hello to a friend who worked in the accounting office. While there, the owner recognized me. "Aren't you Perry Tuttle?" he asked. He was a big Clemson fan. We began talking and he walked me over to a new car. "Why don't you test drive this car we've just brought on the lot?" he said. I wanted to nip this in the bud. "We're not in the market to buy a car," I said firmly. But he insisted. "No, no, just test drive it and tell me what you think," he said.

I hesitated. "Test drive it down the road?" I asked. What did he mean?

"No, no, keep it for a couple of days and then tell me what you think," he said, smiling.

"Okay," I answered. "Sure." I knew I wasn't buying anything.

I brought it back in two days. "Keep it for a little while," he said. So, I brought it back after a week. I thought, something's up. This time when I returned the car, I had a serious talk with him. "Listen, I want to give you your car back," I explained. "We're not going to buy it."

"Perry, you keep this car until I tell you to bring it back," he said. He was just as serious.

Do you know how long I kept that car? Almost a year. I would literally come back once a month. He would say, "Perry, I have cars," and send me home. From that time, since 1992, until today I have driven a new car almost every year. God has unexpectedly provided for us in the most unusual ways. One year it was a BMW, another, an Infinity. We have driven top of the line vehicles since '92. Right now there are three cars in my driveway and I did not pay for any of them.

Because of this experience, we are learning that God is working to improve our faith. The Bible says that Jesus is "the author and perfecter of our faith" (Hebrews 12:2, NIV) and that "he rewards everyone who searches for him" (Hebrews 11:6, CEV). As we believe, He makes that belief stronger. He is perfecting it. He is writing the next chapter.

The world uses money to get things done. If you want to buy a car, you put down U.S. currency. But faith is the currency we put down to acquire what God has for us. We had no idea when we gave Lucy our beautiful new car that God would give us even more cars in the years ahead—more than we could imagine. We didn't expect that. We were just being obedient. The immediate result was an ugly minivan that I hated. But our treasury note in the bank of faith was maturing. God, who loves to reward those who seek Him, was compounding our interests in ways we never imagined. As the years have passed, and our faith has matured, we have cashed out large rewards. If we had held on to that luxury car in 1992, it would seem old and outdated today. The shine would be gone. The thrill would be gone. But the faith we experienced in 1992 has not lost any of its luster. In the years since then, its shine has grown brighter. Thanks be to God that he is the author who writes out the faith He has for us, then perfects it as we begin banking with it.

Our sons need to see that we're trusting in something

bigger than ourselves to fulfill our roles as men. We're tempted to think we've gotten to where we are by our brains or guts or raw talent. "I made it happen," we think. Yet as David said late in life, "riches and glory come from you, you're ruler over all" (I Chronicles 29:12, The Message). Whatever we have—any riches or glory—God has given them. If we can lay hold of this truth, we'll go deep into the heart of faith.

The Spike

Slamming the football in the end zone after a touchdown says it all. The spike drives home the point: We scored! It's a power move that completes the win.

As fathers, there are certain lessons we want to drive so deeply into our sons' hearts that when the time comes, the burn to do the right thing is deep. These spikes cannot be weakened by shifting values in the world or unfamiliar circumstances.

A home in which a son experiences mercy and forgiveness becomes a deep spike in his heart. If he sees his father not just giving mercy, but seeking mercy, the spike penetrates deeper. A man who lives by his conscience, admitting his mistakes, can really have an impact. I have a lot of joy and expectation for some of the dads I know because they are going to reap big rewards down the road. An example is my friend Jimmy, a hunter. He goes to my church and he loves to hunt. Our eight-year-old boys are good friends.

Not long ago Jimmy was out deer hunting with one of his buddies. He had bagged his limit for the day, two deer, when he suddenly had the opportunity to kill a third. In the heat of the moment, as he tells it, a wave of greed swept over him. Boom. Down went the deer.

This man was so convicted by what he did in the woods that he called me. He had no peace. Because I am not a hunter, I asked him, what's the big deal? I had a hard time understanding why he felt so guilty. But for Jimmy, the big deal was that he had done something unethical. He knew it and was under conviction.

That night before dinner, he brought up the matter with

his family. His young son, who practically worships his dad, was devastated. "I'm so disappointed," he said, tears in his eyes as he got up and left the table. I was surprised an eight-year-old would say that.

Jimmy took his medicine and called the game warden in Raleigh. After confessing what he had done, he waited to be told the next step. Would he lose his hunting license? Would he get slapped with a hefty fine? Could you go to jail for something like that?

The game warden was silent. Finally, he said, "We don't get calls like this." Apparently, it takes quite a bit of work to catch someone shooting past their limit. The warden wasn't even sure of the penalty. "Well," he told Jimmy, "just don't do it again."

Jimmy sat there, holding his breath. He was thinking, that's it? That's all you're going to do to me?

That was it.

That spike goes deep. Jimmy's repentance drove a spike down into his son's heart that went so deep, his boy will remember this story even when he is grown. He'll learn that his father is a man who can say, "I'm sorry." A heart like this gives a son a reason to come home.

Grace, mercy, forgiveness. . . these are reasons you can give your son to come home. He has a need to be with you that is powerful. God shows us this need in nature, especially in birds. During World War II, the homing pigeon was famous for its ability to find its way home, even across hundreds of miles over land and water. These humble birds reliably carried thousands of messages for the Allies. To this day, scientists still do not understand how they did it. Homing pigeons are like a metaphor of the unwritten law on the hearts of men: we long for home.

The Bible closes with a picture of our new home. In the revelation that John recorded, there are specific details about our heavenly home. Jesus wanted John to share the news that He was preparing a place for us. He is waiting for our arrival.

Jesus gave us a reason to come home.

Daddies, let's do the same for our boys.

Chapter 7

••••••••••••••••••••••

Fathers, Teach Your Sons
To Be Responsible

"David left his supplies in the care of the quartermaster and ran to the battle line. When he arrived, he asked his brothers how they were. While he was speaking with them, suddenly the champion named Goliath, the Philistine from Gath, came forward from the Philistine battle line and shouted his usual words, which David heard." I Samuel 17:22-24, HCS

    David followed Jesse's instructions to take food to his brothers stationed at the army base. When he got there, he asked the quartermaster to keep an eye on the supplies while he ran to the front lines to find his brothers. Making his way through the crowd of soldiers, he spotted his brothers up at the battle line. As they began to talk, suddenly, in the middle of the conversation, a rumble began across the ravine in the Philistine camp. David looked in the distance and saw a huge warrior moving through the enemy crowd, making his way to their front line. Towering above the other men, he was stunning. David had never seen anything like this. Goliath broke out from the company, walked like a rumbling vision from hell into the clearing, planted his feet and began shouting challenges at the Israel army. The men around David were terrified.

    David wasn't looking for a fight, but a fight showed up. Standing there with his brothers he watched a threat—a mega-man—openly defy the strength and will of his countrymen. Goliath wanted to knock somebody out.

    In the process of following his dad's instructions to take a gift to the field commander, food to his brothers, and to get a report, David witnessed a disturbing scene. Yet he saw it from a safe distance. He could have thought to himself, "I'm a kid. These older guys know more than I do. They'll take care of this." Yet from what we read in I Samuel 17, such a thought never crossed his mind. He was not held back by doubt. Rather than thinking, "Uh, I really don't know what to do here," he thought something more like this: "I don't know what I'm going to do, but I'm going to do *something*. I'll figure it out as

I go." Growing up in the House of Jesse, David had handled enough responsibility to be confident when faced with a blatant threat. Rather than stepping back into the shadows and disappearing, rather than waiting to see what would happen, he stepped out into the light to act.

In the midst of being responsible, of following his dad's orders, he ran into Goliath.

It's a pattern we can relate to. When we are obeying our heavenly Father and following His instructions, we experience opposition. "In this world you will have trouble," Jesus said before going to the cross (John 16:33, NIV). He was preparing His friends for the future.

Fathers, if we want to shape our sons to be giant killers, we start now by training them to handle responsibility, long before they begin visiting the front lines. As they grow up to be responsible young men, they will have the ability and insight to respond appropriately to life's challenges. Instead of their first thoughts being ones of doubt, of "uh oh, I'm in trouble," they'll think, "let me have a shot at this." They're counting on us to get them ready, to tell them what the future looks like. Not all challenges will be clad in bronze and bearing lethal weapons— some may wear skirts or some may fit into a wallet. Some may be ethical challenges; some may be financial challenges. But if our sons are responsible and are doing what's right, they will be tested. A Goliath will show up. In fact, if you, as a dad, are being responsible and doing what's right, Goliaths are showing up in your life. This is the nature of the Christian life.

Locker Room Ties

As a former pro-football player, I know the sweat and discipline that are behind a Monday night football game. It's a lot of fun to flip on the TV on a Monday night, settle into a leather chair, and watch a game. But the guys who play the game know that every pass, every run, every tackle is built on countless hours of practice. For some of us, we may have started practicing for that pro career when we were kids. I started in fourth grade, dreaming of the day I would run a winning touchdown before thousands of cheering fans. Countless choices—probably tens of thousands, actually—took place before I was on the cover of *Sports Illustrated*. There was the choice in seventh grade to show up on a hot August day to train, a choice in tenth grade to keep working on my run, a choice in high school to not talk back to a coach I hated, a choice in college to keep catching until my hands could practically feel the leather coming. Small choices led to bigger choices. One experience paved the way for another.

I mention this because it's easy to focus on the result we want while neglecting the work it takes to get there. It's easy to cheer from the chair. But getting to the big win takes a lot of repetition in things that, seen individually, don't appear to be that important. One more push in the high school weight room or one more run around the track hardly seem related to boarding an Atlanta Falcons plane for a Miami game. But they are. In a similar way, your son gets ready for meeting a Goliath by taking care of ordinary responsibilities. For David, that meant working with his dad's livestock. For your son, it will mean keeping his room clean and learning to pick up after himself. It will mean learning the small courtesies that set a man apart, such as speaking to others with respect, holding a door open, or ordering with ease during a business luncheon. Let's wake up and pay attention to how critical these small matters are to his success in life.

Teaching our sons to be responsible in these things requires patience, practice, and repetition. Sometimes it will seem like we are not making progress. Sometimes it will seem like no matter how much effort we put forth, they're not getting it. Teaching our boys how to do something will take time. We'll have to repeat ourselves. They'll fumble. We'll try again. But with practice, they'll learn the skills they need to handle life.

Have you ever been in a locker room and had to tie a tie with your teammates watching? Were you confident? If you had to guess at what you were doing, you remember the sting of embarrassment. I know a number of men whose fathers never taught them to tie a tie. One friend had so little confidence in this area that he showed up at my house one day with an armful of ties. He didn't want me to teach him, he just wanted me to pre-tie them for him. He wanted to be able to slip one over his head and slide the knot up. "Just get yourself a clip tie," I chided him. His dad had never taken the time to show him how to properly tie a tie. When he needed to do it, he doubted himself. Instead of thinking, "hey, I want a shot at this—teach me how to do it," he thought, "I really don't know what to do here. Can I get somebody else to take care of it?" Don't allow your son to go through life guessing about how to handle his responsibilities. If you do, he'll stumble through life, becoming a young man like the one described in the following letter.

Imagine walking into your office one afternoon after lunch and you see an envelope on your desk. You walk around your chair and pick it up. Opening it, this is what you read . . .

Dear Dad: I Met Your Son Today

Dear Dad—dear entrepreneur Dad, dear six-figure Dad,

I met your son today. I saw him early in the morning. When I reached out my hand and introduced myself, he hesitated, looking down as he shook my hand and I spoke my name. We talked and I invited him to join me for breakfast at a coffee shop. When the waitress came to our table, I saw the clumsiness of how he spoke to her. A little while later she brought out his plate. He picked up his fork and started eating, not noticing that my plate was still on its way from the kitchen. His napkin stayed on the table. When the bill came, he studied the numbers for a second then pulled out some cash. I could see he didn't know how to calculate the tip.

He's nearly a man, Dad, but he's guessing.

After we got into the car, I asked him if he had time to ride with me to a men's clothing store. I needed to pick up a suit. As I was trying on my pants, he wandered to a table of sharp-looking ties. "Go ahead, try one on," I urged him. I saw how embarrassed he felt when I asked him to tie his best tie.

I stood in front of the three-way mirror with the tailor, checking out the fit and length. In the reflection I saw a young lady come into the shop. I heard her say she was there to pick up something for her father. She was attractive and close to your son's age. In the mirror I studied him as he watched her. I could see what was going through his mind. Dad, have you ever talked to him about how to treat a woman?

Dad, I met your son today. We talked, we laughed—he'll soon be a man. But he's got a lot of questions. We ended our day at a restaurant. As we entered through the glass doors, he stepped in front of an older woman, an executive in a suit. At the table, I saw his anger when his food didn't come on time. And even though I paid for his meal, he forgot to thank me.

Get Started

I'm very fortunate to be married to Loretta. She understands the value of obedience better than any woman I have ever known. Loretta understands how important it is to teach our children to be responsible. She has insight into each of their personalities and has educated herself about their different learning styles. Loretta has been a constant source of encouragement to me. She has reminded me that, ultimately, the results are in God's hands. Our job is to provide faithful instruction.

Dads, in order to teach your sons to be responsible, you and your bride must start working with them at a very young age. You are a team. As I told my children, "Your mother and I were a family before you ever arrived. You are a welcome addition to our family, but that is all you are. I love Loretta more than I love all of you. The two of us started this family. We *are* a family."

The first place to start is by teaching your sons to clean up. This is something that takes patient supervision, and the weight of it—if your wife is home during the day—will fall on her. She is going to need your support and leadership. Loretta has patiently worked with our children, starting at very young ages, to handle responsibilities around the house. At two years of age our children put socks on their hands to wipe down the baseboards. Loretta will practice making a bed with one of them for weeks. She works with them until she is sure they can do it well. "They don't have a frame of reference for what we ask of them," she says to me. We know what a made-up bed looks like because we have been working on one for thirty or forty years. But your little boy has never taken a close look at a smooth bedspread, a turned-down sheet, or pillow that has been straightened up. You can't just order your kids to do something, showing them once or twice what you mean. They'll need to practice again and again.

Your children should also be responsible, at a very young age, to address adults with a title. Whether you teach them to say "Mr. Smith" or "Mr. John," they should use a title when addressing adults. They are learning to give out value to the people around them. Their response is just as important when an adult addresses them. "Yeah" or "uh huh" are sloppy answers that become habit forming.

You may think your children are not capable of learning these things, but even babies have a high level of intelligence. Loretta and I have seen very young children manipulate their parents, yet the parents are convinced their children are not smart enough to follow their instructions. One afternoon in our neighborhood, a mom cornered me about her son who spends a lot of time at our house. "Whenever he talks about you and Loretta, he always says, 'Mr. Perry' or 'Mrs. Loretta.' I don't understand—I can't get him to address any other adult by 'Mr.' or 'Mrs.' What's the secret?" I smiled as I thought about her son. I had recently spoken to him about helping himself to our refrigerator without asking first. "When he's at our house, we expect the same behavior from him that we ask of our own children," I said. I knew this mom's son was willing, but no one was showing him what to do. Kids have to learn, through repetition, how to be a responsible guest.

Writing 101

Part of teaching our children to be responsible is to teach them to notice and acknowledge the gifts and sacrifices of others. Learning to say "thank you" in a meaningful way takes skill and time. One of the best ways to do it is by writing a letter or sending a card. Such a note should be personal.

The Bible gives us excellent examples of how to write thank you notes—just read David's psalms of praise and thanksgiving to God. The more specific your children can be in giving thanks, the more meaningful it will be to the person receiving it. Compare it to telling your wife you love her. What would she rather hear: "I love you" or "I love you because..."? When we take the time to go beyond what's expected, we not only bless others, but we become blessed. Our appreciation of them deepens. Our hearts are enlarged. We slow down and think about things.

This is where we want to take our boys.

Here's how a friend of mine recently applied this to his situation. He went out and bought about twenty different thank you cards, picking them out himself. He also bought six pens. Then one night after dinner, he and his family cleared the table and he spread out the cards. "We're going to spend the next twenty or thirty minutes writing thank you cards," he told them. One of his sons had been awarded a full basketball scholarship to a prestigious college. His assignment was to write a thank you note to his high school coach. Here is how his dad directed him: "Tell your coach how you were before he began coaching you. Next, tell him what you learned from him. Be specific. Then end with the results. 'Because you coached me I am now. . .' and you fill in the blank. Are you ready to play college ball? Why? How has he prepared you to go further?"

Cracking the Code

During World War II there was a heated effort on every side to break secret radio codes that directed troops and ships. The signals were out there, but no one could understand them. One of the biggest successes came in 1942 when the Americans figured out Japan's messages and trumped her plans for the naval battle of Midway. Thanks to "Magic," the name of the American operation, the Japanese—not the Americans—were the ones taken by surprise. Many historians consider the American victory at Midway the most important naval battle of the war. America's inferior fleet whipped the Japanese, all because we got the right information. We broke the code.

When I look back on my high school and college years, I realize that I guessed my way through much of my life. I guessed with dating, I guessed at finances, I even guessed at college. Everything I faced seemed to be a multiple-choice question. I look back on the men in my life, both in college and in high school, and each one left me guessing. They knew better—I know they knew better because life had not worked out for them the way they thought it would. As a young man I was like a radio operator during World War II. I heard a lot of signals over the airwaves, but they didn't make sense. There were codes that I didn't understand.

Our sons are hearing the jumbled signals of manhood. They need a father to translate for them.

Dads, it is so important for us to hand down our information to our boys. It is so vital for them to hear, to understand, and to be blessed. It was Jesse's responsibility to not only send David off to his brothers with supplies, but to also explain to him what he was thinking. "I'm concerned about my boys," I can hear him telling David. "Your brothers may be tired—they haven't been home in months. It's dangerous out there. You take them this food and let them know I'm thinking about them. Tell them I am praying for them. Then bring back word on how they are."

Let's bring our sons in on our thinking. We want to bless them. We want to crack the code of manhood for them and explain it. In the same way that our Lord told his followers, "in this world you will have trouble," we want our followers, our sons, to know what the world is like. We want them to step into manhood ready to meet the challenges they'll encounter.

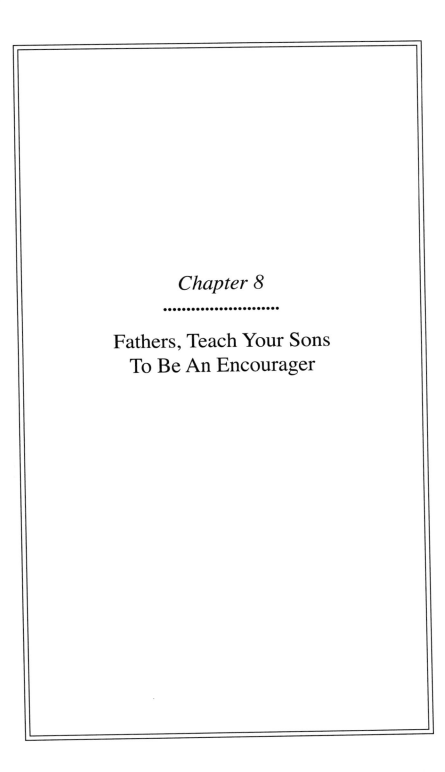

Chapter 8

....

Fathers, Teach Your Sons
To Be An Encourager

"David said to Saul, 'Let no one lose heart on account of this Philistine; your servant will go and fight him." I Samuel 17:32

A man will lose heart if he thinks he is headed for defeat. The Bible says that Saul and his men "were terrified and deeply shaken" (I Samuel 17:11, NLT). Because of fear, they had lost confidence in their ability to fight back. They had given up hope in God's victory. Yet David saw their condition and spoke words that gave them courage. His words were powerful because they promised action. "Let no one lose heart on account of this Philistine," he said, *"your servant will go and fight him."* David did more than say something encouraging; he stepped to the front of the line. His courage to do something got everyone's attention.

A few paragraphs later, we read about a very different group of soldiers than those described at the beginning of this story. The same men who cowered for forty days as Goliath challenged them became men who chased down a fight. As Goliath fell, the Philistine soldiers probably stepped back in disbelief, stumbling over each other. Moments later, they were running for cover. David's brothers and the other soldiers looked across the ravine at what was happening and let out a war cry. Then they took off, chasing them for miles. The adrenaline must have been incredible. "When the Philistines saw what had happened to their hero, they started running away. But the soldiers of Israel and Judah let out a battle cry and went after them as far as Gath and Ekron. The bodies of the Philistines were scattered all along the road from Shaaraim to Gath and Ekron. When the Israelite army returned from chasing the Philistines, they took what they wanted from the enemy camp" (I Samuel 17:51-53, CEV).

An Encourager Sees Two Realities

David had the courage to face Goliath because he saw something bigger than Goliath; he saw God. Goliath was the flesh-and-blood reality, but God was the bigger unseen reality. An encourager sees God and shows Him to us. An encourager has two sets of eyes.

A number of years ago I had the opportunity to meet one of the most powerful banking CEOs in the country. I had retired from football and was in business. I knew that this man had the influence to make or break my career. He had arranged for me to meet him in the skyscraper restaurant at his corporate headquarters. As I prepared for the meeting, I struggled to find my balance. This was a big break for me and I didn't want to blow it. I began to think through what I wanted to say and how I would say it.

I needed some counsel.

My good friend Jeff Davis lived in Tampa, so I called him to see if I could fly down and spend a couple of days with him prior to the meeting. I wanted time to talk to Jeff, to hear his counsel, and to pray together. He was free, so I immediately booked a ticket. I found a bargain flight for $268 and headed south.

I arrived at the Tampa airport late one morning and Jeff met me at the gate. I just couldn't wait to spend two days with him. We were roommates in college and had walked through so much together. I knew it would be good to pray and talk together about this upcoming event.

As we were walking through the airport we came to a coffee shop. "Stop—let's get a cup of coffee," Jeff said. Airport coffee isn't high on my list, so I answered him, "Let's go to your house—I'm ready to get out of this airport." But he insisted. "No, let's just sit and have a cup of coffee."

We sat down in the airport coffee shop and Jeff leaned back in his chair. "So, tell me about this meeting," he said. I began to talk. As I told him all about this man—his reputation, what he had accomplished, his net worth, his influence—Jeff brought a pen out of the jacket he was wearing. While I talked he took the cap off the pen and held the point out, placing his thumb at the very end so that just the tip was showing. This was distracting.

Suddenly, out of nowhere, he said, "You don't know who God is."

"What are you doing?" I asked him. He seemed preoccupied with the pen. "I'm sorry," he said, "what were you saying?" So I continued.

I had not gotten much further when he said it again. "You don't know who God is, do you?" he asked. "What?" I said. I was starting to get ticked off. I always call him Roomie, a holdover from college days. I said, "Roomie, what are you doing?" Again he said it: "You don't know who God is."

"I do know who God is," I answered him, defensively. "Tell me who God is," he replied. I gave him some really nice scripture verses. Then he said, "Now tell me about this guy again? I'm sorry, I got sidetracked." So I went back and picked up where I left off. By this point I was annoyed. I didn't want to hear any more questions.

Jeff interrupted me again. "You don't know who God is. Let me tell you what happened to me a couple of weeks ago." Frustrated, I got quiet and listened.

"Joanie and I went on a cruise. There are some people who have a private plane and they flew us down to the end of Miami. When we arrived to board the ship, at the plank leading up from the dock, I looked to the right and couldn't see the end of the ship. I looked to the left and couldn't see the end of it. And I looked up—five stories high. Tut, it was so high, I couldn't believe how high it was."

He gave me a long look then said, "You don't know who God is." I waited.

"For four days we were on that ship. We couldn't even swim in all the swimming pools. And they fed us, oh, it was awesome."

Studying the tip of his pen, he continued. "When the cruise was over, we docked and got off the ship to board this little plane again. It was just a little plane, a crop duster. As we went up, we began to see just how big that ship really was. From the air we could see the whole thing. Tut, the higher we flew, the smaller that ship got. We got so high that the ship finally looked like this," he said, and with that, he held up the pen, barely showing the tip of it with his thumb.

"Where God is, that is what that ship looks like. That's what this guy you're worried about looks like. That's what the bank he runs looks like. You," he paused, "you don't know who God is." I just stared at him.

"Your problem is not the CEO," Jeff said. "Your problem is God. He's too small. Get back on the plane and go home."

You know how long that meeting lasted? No more than fifteen minutes. I paid $268 for a fifteen-minute meeting. Jeff got up and we said goodbye. I spent two hours waiting for the next flight, thinking about what he said.

Jeff was my encourager—he showed me a bigger reality. God my Father, who formed me and knitted me together in my mother's womb, who chose me to follow Him, who gave His son for me—this God was living and working in me for His glory. He had placed His value inside of me; His favor was Christ in me. Jeff's words had struck home. He spoke truth to me, a truth that encouraged me to look up.

When David went out to meet Goliath, he wasn't staring at his five stones and slingshot, wondering how everything would work out. He wasn't looking down at what he held in his hands. David was looking up; past Goliath, past the ravine, past the soldiers lined up behind Goliath, past the armor bearer marching before Goliath. Something bigger than all of that had captured David's imagination. David was seeing his God.

An Encourager Speaks Truth

To encourage someone is to give them hope. At the core of hope is truth. Because there is so little truth given to our boys today—whether from society, their families or their friends—they are looking for it in dead-end places. They become confused, dismayed and hurt when those things don't satisfy. They have bought into a lie—that you can build yourself up apart from truth. In the end, this stings.

Let your son know that the next car, the next friend, the next cell phone or video game, the next trip, the next cute girl, the next vacation—whatever it is he wants—will not give him the truth he needs. Help him to understand his soul. How many men do you know who are still looking for satisfaction? How many keep taking a detour from life, thinking *the next time* will be it? That they will find something that holds their attention, something that will last?

I mentioned that I am the chaplain for an NBA team. I recently met with a group from the team for a chapel service. There were ten of us—nine millionaires and me. One of the men is worth hundreds of millions. We were sitting in a group and I pulled out a hundred dollar bill from my wallet. "Guys, I'm going to do something," I said. "I will give you a hundred dollars if you will do ten push-ups in ten seconds." They were ready to get down. One of the guys quickly did the ten and I handed him the bill. "It's yours," I said.

He took it and didn't look too closely at it. He was sitting right beside me. I had him turn the bill over. It was the same on both sides. It wasn't real.

"Satan is like that," I explained. "He'll ask you to do things to get a lot of money. Later, you will honestly say, 'I can't believe I did that.' This money—this currency that is so important to us—is what we are going to walk on in heaven. God's economy is opposite of our economy. We value gold, but God is going to use it to build sidewalks.

"There will come a day when you say, 'Is that it?' When you have worked hard to get a lot of money only to find out that is not what you were looking for. We need to get to the end of ourselves now."

I can speak from personal experience when I talk to these men. I can relate to their ambition and drive. In a similar way, we can speak to our sons from our personal experience; we can tell them about how God has come through in our lives. Share your stories with your boy. Give him truth you have tested through the things you have been through.

Our sons will learn how to really encourage others when they understand that truth is at the heart of encouragement. When that truth is something they have personally tested, it will be powerful.

David told Saul, "The Lord who delivered me from the paw of the lion and the paw of the bear will deliver me from the hand of this Philistine" (I Samuel 17:37, NIV). David wasn't being prideful or putting his confidence in himself. He did not have illusions about his abilities. He was simply stating fact. A skilled marksman and fighter, he had personally witnessed God's hand on him when he fought. God had rescued him before; God would rescue him now. There was credibility to his claim.

Saul was so encouraged by what David said that the king sent him out to represent the entire nation. Think of the risk Saul was taking. If David failed, the victory went to the Philistines. Saul would face terrible consequences. He and his nation would become slaves to a despised enemy. If his life were spared, he would be known forever as a fool. But David's words outweighed all of these fears. They gave him hope. In a way that this story doesn't explain in detail, Saul recognized truth in David's words. This impression was so strong that he risked becoming a laughingstock to his men. He turned the fate of his country over to a ruddy-faced farm boy.

When God is inside of us, a rock and a slingshot are all we need.

An Encourager Uses "Up" Words

The words we speak to our sons are powerful. The Bible says, "the tongue has the power of life and death" (Proverbs 18:21, NIV). With our tongues we can bring our boys down or we can lift them up. We can speak life into them or we can speak death. An encourager uses words that speak life.

Sometimes we don't think about what we are saying to our sons. Maybe we are playing with them or horsing around and something comes out of our mouths. Words are like arrows—they fly into the heart and stay there. I've let words come out of my mouth that I later regretted.

About three years ago I was playing chess with one of my boys. I love chess; he does, too. I beat him really badly during this game.

We were only going to play one match, but because I beat him so badly he wanted to play again. I told him, no, we were not going to play anymore. He began to plead—come on dad, come on! But I told him, "Son, I beat you and I'm not playing anymore."

He got kind of ticked off, so I poked fun at him, that I beat him. Tears started welling up in his eyes and he began to beg. "Let's play again," he whined. That got all over me.

"Son," I said—I was sharp with him—"don't start crying on me! Stop being a sissy."

Tears started running down his face.

That was it. "Son, don't be a sissy—go to your room," I ordered him.

I left to run an errand. On the way back home, about a mile from my house, traffic was backed up due to construction. I needed to vacuum my car so I pulled into a car wash, hoping the traffic would clear up by the time I finished. But there was still a long line when I got done with the vacuuming, so I parked my car, got out and began to walk. Because of the construction, there were rocks everywhere—big boulders with red mud all over them. As I looked at this mess, all of a sudden, what I had said to my son an hour-and-a-half earlier came ringing into my ears. In an instant it dawned on me that one day, when my boy is twenty-one or twenty-five or thirty, he's going to have a major failure in life, whether in business or college or in a relationship. At that moment, Satan will lean into his ear and say to him, "Remember when you were twelve years old and your dad called you a big sissy? Hey—your dad was right." I froze, gripped by the shock of that thought. The Holy Spirit showed me, in a fast forward moment, that my enemy would use my very words one day to tear my son down.

I wouldn't be there to stop him.

I stared at the boulders under my feet. Leaning over, I picked up a rock, a muddy piece broken off of a giant boulder. Walking to the car, I put it in my trunk and drove home. In my back yard I washed it down with the garden hose, scrubbing it with a brush and drying it with a towel. Then I took a marker and wrote out my son's name on the rock, addressing it like a letter. Then I wrote these words: "This rock has been here a long time. This rock can never outlast my love for you." I added the date and the name of the street where I found the rock. Then I went in the house and put it on his pillow. That night, when he walked in his room to go to bed, those words met him. The rock became a doorkeeper to his room, something he walks by every day, a reminder of my commitment to him.

Daddy, if we want our sons to become encouragers, we must lead the way. When we fail to speak well, let's repent quickly. Let us be men who are committed to speaking "up" words to our boys.

An Encourager Sees Potential

If you have read the book of Esther in the Bible, then you know about her uncle Mordecai. This man was an encourager. His words to young Esther influenced history.

Esther was a queen, married to a man who ruled the ancient world from India to east Africa. This king unwittingly signed the death warrant for all Jews throughout his kingdom, not realizing his wife, Esther, was a Jew. When Mordecai found out about this, he sent a messenger to his niece, pressing her to intercede and speak to her husband. Mordecai and Esther were close because he had raised her after her parents died, and had officially adopted her. She sent a message back explaining that, depending on the king's mood, she could be killed for initiating such a conversation. She was afraid.

When she hesitated, Mordecai sent her this message: "Do not think in your heart that you will escape in the king's palace any more than all the other Jews. For if you remain completely silent at this time, relief and deliverance will arise for the Jews from another place, but you and your father's house will perish. Yet who knows whether you have come to the kingdom for such a time as this?" (Esther 4:13-14, NKJV)

Mordecai understood where Esther's fears were taking her. He could see what would happen if she chose not to act. Like a loving father, he first exposed her faulty thinking. He had a good idea of what was going through her mind and he uncovered it: "Do not think in your heart that you will escape," he warned. Then he directed her attention to the big picture, giving her hope to see her potential. He invited his cherished niece to consider her destiny. He asked her, "Who knows whether you have come to the kingdom for such a time as this?" He wisely gave her a question that only she could answer.

Daddy, when your son is afraid, don't ignore his fears. If you think you know what he is thinking, bring it out into the light. Then ask him a question only he can answer. Help him to consider his God-chosen destiny. Mordecai encouraged his adopted niece to believe great things about her God, and great things about her own life. In the next sentence we read that she decided to speak to the king. Her uncle's words encouraged her to face her fears. He inspired her to see the potential of her destiny. Even if she faced death, she now had the courage she needed. Like Esther, our sons may not need a change of circumstances, but the courage to face the circumstances they are in.

Sometimes what our sons need from us is a picture of the future, described in our own words. From our vantage point, we can see they have a unique role to play in their own generation, just as Esther had a role that was beyond Mordecai's influence. As fathers we can ask them questions that only they can answer, questions that penetrate the heart, that prick the conscience. We can describe the bigger reality, speak truth from our own experience, and then call them, as young men, to consider their potential.

"Follow my example as I follow the example of Christ," Paul said (I Corinthians 11:1, NIV). As we encourage our sons, we teach them the skills to encourage others. Just as David left the House of Jesse with the ability to see the fears in others and speak life, we want to teach our sons to do the same. We want to raise men who understand how to encourage others, not with human ideas, which will blow away, but with words and actions that are powerful, that cut straight to the core.

"The weapons we fight with," Paul wrote, "are not the weapons of the world. On the contrary, they have divine power to demolish strongholds" (II Corinthians 10:4, NIV). Fear is one of the biggest strongholds any of us faces; it is what the soldiers around David were dealing with. David pulled out a weapon that demolished their fear, he encouraged them. Let's teach our sons to be encouragers, men who use the divine power of truth as a weapon against fear, men who know how to give courage to those around them.

Chapter 9

••••••••••••••••••••••

Fathers, Teach Your Sons
To Kill The Lion And The Bear

"But David said to Saul, 'Your servant has been keeping his father's sheep. When a lion or a bear came and carried off a sheep from the flock, I went after it, struck it and rescued the sheep from its mouth. When it turned on me, I seized it by its hair, struck it and killed it. Your servant has killed both the lion and the bear; this uncircumcised Philistine will be like one of them, because he has defied the armies of the living God.'"
I Samuel 17:34-36, NIV

Saul was skeptical of young David's ability to go up against Goliath. To prove his skill, David gave Saul a detailed description of how he killed the two biggest threats to his flock: a lion and a bear. If you read the account closely, David did not grab these wild animals until he had first rescued the sheep. Is it possible that his first strike was from a distance, with a stone from the sling? If the lion was temporarily dazed, I can imagine David running up and pushing the sheep from its jaws, then it regaining consciousness and attacking him. "When it turned on me, I seized it by its hair, struck it and killed it." If this is what happened, then David used the same tactic on Goliath. It explains why he ran up to Goliath after he had fallen and immediately cut off his head.

These stories got Saul's attention. Killing a lion and a bear at close range gave convincing proof that David had the courage to attack Goliath and finish the job.

The Bible invites us to learn from its stories. Paul wrote, "everything that was written in the past was written to teach us" (Romans 15:4, NIV). This part of David's conversation with Saul—the story of how he killed wild animals with his bare hands—is recorded for a reason. God has something to teach us about how to get ready for a Goliath, and it is related to killing a lion and a bear. As I meditate on this story, the lion and bear become metaphors to me, representing two threats to our progress as warriors. They symbolize two things we much teach our boys to kill.

The Lion of Laziness

He may be the king of the jungle, but did you know that a lion sleeps or rests up to twenty hours a day? Or that a lion will give up a chase if it lasts more than fifty to a hundred yards? Did you know that many young lions die because their parents won't hunt enough to feed them?

As powerful and deadly as a lion is, to me he is a symbol of laziness. He will lie around in the brush, neglecting the obvious needs around him. Yet when he springs to life, he kills. Laziness is like that. It stares through half-open eyes at things begging for attention. It doesn't act, so things die. It's so passive it seems harmless, until it is too late.

We must teach our sons to put to death a tendency towards laziness. If we don't, that lion will prowl around them, looking for an opportunity to pick off something of value. Our boys will lose what they own, or the talents entrusted to them, one small resource at a time. There is a lesson to be learned in the fact that a lion doesn't kill a whole flock at once, but picks off the strays, one at a time.

Although laziness may be sleeping in the brush most of the time, when it wakes up hungry, it is deadly. Laziness creeps up, unnoticed and silent, and then takes an easy kill. It slinks away with its prey before anyone realizes something is missing.

One of the strongest areas of laziness that I see in young men today is in learning. Young men are not applying themselves to learn the practical matters of life, such as how to treat a young lady or even how to be good stewards of money and possessions. The world is teaching them to place their self-esteem in ignorance, not achievement. Over ten years ago Charles Sykes wrote a book titled, *Dumbing Down Our Kids: Why American Children Feel Good about Themselves, but Can't Read, Write, or Add* (St. Martin's Press, 1995). Sykes, a researcher who writes on education and other social topics, addressed a unique American problem: Our kids feel good about what they know even though they don't know much.

Their confidence in themselves, or self-esteem, is not based on real achievements as David's was, but on how they feel. It has been widely reported that when American students are tested by international standards, they are high in self-confidence but low in scores. In the International Mathematics and Science Study of 2003, which tested eighth-grade students around the world in math and science, the scores of American students were well below those of Asian countries, and even below those of students in Estonia, Latvia, and the Slovak Republic. As Sykes noted in his list of rules, basing your self-esteem on how you feel is the reverse of the way the world actually operates. "The world won't care about your self-esteem. The world will expect you to accomplish something before you feel good about yourself," he wrote.

What You Don't Know Can Hurt You

If it weren't for *CliffsNotes*, I don't think I would have gotten through college. I had no desire to read or to make an effort to study books. However, when I gave my life to the Lord, that changed. I wanted to know about everything! My perspective changed when I began to see how much there was to know and learn about God. The way I looked at the world changed, too, for I began to see that all around me was His creation. Everyday things became more interesting, and I started to enjoy learning. Today I am filled with curiosity about many different things. When my lawnmower broke recently and I had to take it apart to find the loose belt, I actually enjoyed fixing it. It was almost like hitting a hole-in-one for me!

In college, I was lazy about learning. Ignorance is often the result of laziness. As God's men, we should be constantly learning, and sharing what we learn with others. If we are living our lives in front of a TV, what kind of example are we setting? There are too many exciting things that God wants to teach us to spend our time being lazy. If we want our sons to learn, then we must set the example.

God created us to be learners. From the Old Testament through the New, there is an emphasis on learning. Moses challenged the people to "learn" the laws (Deuteronomy 5:1), to "learn" how to honor God (14:23), and to "learn" how to fear him (31:13). Jesus said, "learn from me" (Matthew 11:29). He used the natural world to explain important things, such as "learn this lesson from the fig tree" (Mark 13:28). And Paul wrote constantly about the opportunities we have, as Christians, to learn.

Let your son inside your inner circle. Tell him stories and ask him questions. If he is older, talk to him while you are riding in a car; if he is young, get on the floor with him and tell him a story. Depending on his age, you will be his coach or his counselor. Challenge his thinking. Help him to learn through successes. If you don't, the failures he will experience out of ignorance will create a backward lifestyle. Don't underestimate the valuable lessons you can teach your son as you talk to him about your own life. Ask God to give you insight into his life, so that you can share stories with him that capture his attention and imagination.

Our culture has made it easy for our boys to study things that have little eternal value. The values of our world run counter to the values of Christ. "The Scripture declares that the whole world is a prisoner of sin," Paul wrote the Galatians (3:22). We all know what kind of values are promoted by the mainstream media, but according to a 2005 study on media in the lives of kids, we're not doing much about it. "A typical 8- to 18-year-old lives in a home containing three TV sets, three CD/tape players, three radios, three VCR/DVD players, two video game consoles, and a computer" (*Generation M: Media in the Lives of 8-18 Year-olds,* A Kaiser Family Foundation Study, March 2005). This same report notes that more than half of all 7th-12th grade kids say there are no family rules governing the use of the TV, computer, video games or music. There have got to be some Christians in that mix. In most American homes, the TV is on most of the time, even when no one is watching. Most of our boys love video games and computer games and the same report found that they are playing them at unprecedented rates. They're getting over four hours a day of "screen exposure"—whether from the computer, TV, DVDs, videos or movies. That does not include screen exposure at school.

These habits influence our sons' creativity, not to mention their health. TV has fostered a lazy attitude in boys, keeping them from being creative. But it isn't just television that is helping them to be lazy. As parents, we are contributing to the problem by doing things for them that they should be doing for themselves. We're also not teaching them the knowledge they need to act with confidence. As a result, they don't know how to take initiative. One area where this is particularly troubling is in their relationships with the opposite sex. Girls ask them out, call them on their cell phones, and drive them around.

In 1937 cartoonist Al Capp came up with a race for his Li'l Abner comic strip. The worried father of one of ugliest girls in Dogpatch announced that a race would be held in which the unmarried girls would chase the town's bachelors. Those who caught their man got to marry him. His homely daughter, Sadie Hawkins, caught her victim and became a bride. Within a few years, hundreds of colleges across America were holding Sadie Hawkins Day dances, encouraging young ladies to do the asking.

A silly comic strip from the 1930s illustrates a lot of what is taking place in the world today: young women chasing men. The problem, however, is not just the young women. It's the dads. We need to teach our sons to not get in that race. God has a better one for them, one in which they are the initiators and are confident about becoming a husband.

Dads, laziness is a killer. It may seem harmless—lounging around taking phone calls or spending hours on video games—but don't be deceived. "The whole world is under the control of the evil one," John wrote (I John 5:19). We can encourage our sons to get out from under that control by learning great things about life. It takes effort to "keep oneself from being polluted by the world" (James 1:27). Set the example by making the effort. Be a learner yourself.

And Then There's the Bear

It's been estimated that a bear's sense of smell is seven times greater than that of a bloodhound, a dog that has been called a nose with feet. Bloodhounds can pick up a scent that is more than four days old and can follow it for over a hundred miles. A bear can detect a scent from a mile away. If he's after something, he can move at thirty-five miles per hour.

When you pass through a place, you leave a scent. As you move ahead, an invisible trail—a smell—connects your past to your present. If a predator crosses that scent, even though it's history, he can track you down.

To kill the bear symbolizes, to me, putting to death the unfinished business of the past. I believe God calls us to go back and make things right, to the best of our ability. If we don't, those things will leave a smell that may, eventually, cause a bear to follow us. Maybe we need to go back and ask for forgiveness from someone. Maybe we need to admit a wrong that never came to light. I cannot tell you what this looks like for you. All I know is that I have seen, repeatedly, the problems that unfinished business can cause. If we want our sons to live with a clear conscience then we can lead the way by having one ourselves.

Who is the bear that will use this information against us? The Bible calls Satan the "accuser of the brethren." That is his job. That is what he does. If you don't hear from God about an issue from your past, you will hear from Satan. I recently spent time with someone who has been in the ministry for many years, and has been richly blessed by God. But he was in a mental hospital, feeling abandoned by the Lord. In the midst of this terrible experience, he confessed a sin that had troubled him for over twenty years, and which he never told anyone about. If you don't deal with your past then when tough times come, Satan will bring it up. He is your adversary. He is against you. However, your friends in Christ are your brothers. Talk to them about what concerns you, pray with them, and ask for counsel. "Love covers a multitude of sins" (I Peter 4:8). As hard as it may be to bring it up, God heard about it a long time ago. His love, in the hearts of your friends, will take you to a deeper level of grace. A man who knows he is a sinner is not likely to judge you. As you experience God's mercy in such a friends, you will be strengthened to kill the bear.

If you don't deal with your past and it surfaces one day, something unfortunate may happen. The church is populated with people who don't really understand the grace of God or the fact that they are still sinners. As a result, when Satan launches his attack, those who should have been a part of your healing process become your adversaries. For these people, if you screw up one time, that's it. It's sad. The church really pounces on the wounded. This attitude can take root not only in the congregation, but also in the church leadership. I remember walking into an elders meeting, years ago, in the midst of small talk and chitchat. The theme of the conversation was sin, and I was hearing a lot of self-righteous talk. I interrupted them to say, "I think I need to go on record sharing some of my stuff." I began to tell them some of the things of my past. That put a chill on their talk, which was really boasting. I want to be like Paul who wrote, "May I never boast except in the cross of our Lord Jesus Christ" (Galatians 4:16). I did not want to participate in a conversation that brought others down. Let's not bring others down, but bring Christ up.

We can develop open relationships with other men by being honest ourselves and by asking questions. I asked a friend in the ministry, "If God chooses to raise you up, what is the one thing from your past that Satan could bring up at the height of your success? What is the one thing that God, Satan, and you know about that, if made public, could become your undoing?"

"You're the first person to ever ask me that," he said,

amazed. After we talked he said, "You're the first person I've ever told." He felt liberated. He felt safe. He had a strategy. You, too, could talk to one or two trusted friends and tell them about the one thing that would hurt or possibly destroy the people you love.

Once you have killed that bear, you become a safe place for other men to turn to. It's like you become a point man, a man like Mr. Russell.

I met Mr. Russell early one morning when I was out house hunting. I drove by a house that was for sale, so I pulled into the driveway to get the phone number off the sign. It was around 7 a.m., but I decided to call the number and leave a message. To my surprise, a man answered the phone. Even more to my surprise, the man was inside the house. He was a Realtor and he had listed his own home. He invited me to come in and have a look. I got out of my car and went to the door where I was greeted by an elderly gentleman—both he and his wife were dressed and ready for the day even though the hour was early.

After walking around the property with Mr. Russell, I was intrigued by him. As I was leaving, I turned to him and said, "Mr. Russell, what is your story?"

"Story?" he asked, looking puzzled.

"Yes sir. Every man has a story. What is your story?"

He began to talk. "Well, I was fighting in Normandy—in France," he said. "I was a point."

I didn't know what that meant. "A point? What is that?" I asked.

"I was the point man in my platoon. My job was this: I was expendable. Because of my fellow soldiers, I went out with a gun and I shot where I thought the enemy was. My job was to draw fire."

As I listened to this man, eighty-something years old, he showed me where he was shot, near his suspenders.

"I was the guy who drew fire. As soon as the enemy shot, my fellow soldiers knew where the enemy was. I knew I was going to get shot, I knew I was going to get killed.

That was my job."

Incredibly, Mr. Russell survived World War II.

Later, as I thought about his story, I thought about the spiritual point men in the body of Christ. They step in front of their fellow soldiers and draw out Satan's fire, enabling their brothers to identify his location. It may be very painful to step into that spot—the point man may hear things he doesn't want to hear, or feel things that are uncomfortable—but by stepping out, he saves lives. When we step between a brother and Satan and invite our brother to share his past with us, we draw out Satan's fire. Our brother can see where Satan is hiding. He can fire against that bear.

Killing the bear of the past brings everything under the lordship of Christ. It diffuses the power of secrets. It makes us humble, which, ironically, then lifts us up. We want to be men who are transparent but tactful, honest but discreet. We should go back and ask for forgiveness from those we have wronged, and help others do the same. Let's not leave any unfinished business behind us.

A Father's Role

As I look back at the scripture that began this chapter, I wonder how David learned to kill the lion and the bear. Did Jesse teach him? Or did he learn it from his older brothers, who must have been taught by their father when he was a younger man? Jesse would not have sent David out to protect and shepherd the flock without making sure he had the skills he needed. A father does not put his son in harm's way unless he is confident he is ready for the challenge. Jesse judged David to be ready.

Sometimes we must have a lot of patience as our boys learn a skill. Jesse was probably no different. Is it possible that Jesse was patient with David, waiting for him to learn to strike back? Perhaps it took David awhile to learn how to kill the lion and the bear. Maybe he did not act the first time it happened— did he watch the herd dwindle down over a period of months, finally deciding that enough was enough? Did his father allow him to feel the pressure of failure, to feel the losses? Isn't that how God deals with us? Did Jesse have faith in his son, riding out the losses, believing that David would finally connect his skills with his passion?

Jesse allowed David to be tested. Without a challenge, David could not have learned how to fight. Jesse put him in that situation, making sure he was tested in private before he was tested in public. He won a victory over wild animals before he won a victory over a man.

We, too, must look for situations that will test our sons so that they can become skilled in their own right.
By allowing David to fight his own fights, Jesse gave him the chance to build a history. Through personal experience, David learned what he could do. And he also found out where God would show up. We know that he had fears and apprehensions just like any man. In the psalms we read that he dealt with anxiety and discouragement, despair and weakness. David was a hero, but he was human.

Our sons are human, and they have the potential to become heroes.

David was prepared for Goliath because he experienced success against a lion and a bear, killers that hid in the normal landscape of life. As fathers, let's tell our sons about the threats they can expect, and then make sure they learn how to effectively kill those things that will maul their fruitfulness or steal their future prosperity. By faith, we can send them out to take care of significant responsibilities, knowing that success in their young years will prepare them for great things in the future.

Chapter 10

••••••••••••••••••••••

Fathers, Give Your Son A Reason
To Be Proud You Are His Daddy

"'Tell me about your father, my boy,' Saul said. And David replied, 'His name is Jesse, and we live in Bethlehem.'" I Samuel 17:58, NLT

The defeat of Goliath—a story that is probably the most famous war story in history and one that has been told to young boys for thousands of years—ends with one significant question: "Tell me about your father, my boy."

This is where our journey ends. Daddy, as we come to the close of this book, would you consider how your son will answer that question? What reason will you give him to be proud of you?

For many years, people have asked for my autograph. If my children are with me, they are impressed because they see I am important in the eyes of others. At Clemson University, my alma mater, I am treated like a celebrity. Strangers walk up to introduce themselves. People I know bring their friends by to say hello. In a stadium filled with 80,000 fans, I am invited to sit in the president's box. Because I was a first-team All American receiver and all-time Clemson leader in career receptions, I have a history that others respect. I've been designated one of the school's top football players of all time by a panel of Clemson historians. All of this recognition puts my children a little in awe of me. When people ask them, "Who is your daddy?" they love to answer, "I am Perry Tuttle's son" or "I am Perry Tuttle's daughter." Wearing a bright orange jersey with my name across the back and number twenty-two on the front, they know they stand out. They are proud to be noticed as one of my children.

We probably have little idea of how important our reputation is to our children. Because we love them, we think far more about the pride they bring us—or perhaps the occasional embarrassment—than we do about how they feel towards us. "I'm so proud of you" are words we work hard to tell them. It is less common, however, to hear a child say,

"Dad, I'm proud of you." Yet we read in Proverbs 17:6 that "parents are the pride of their children." The man who wrote those words was David's son and Jesse's grandson, Solomon. He knew from firsthand experience how it felt for a kid to be proud of his dad. He certainly was proud of his.

Because children are immature, it is easy to impress them. A son may be proud of his father because of how much money he makes or because of his titles and achievements or because of the way others address him. If we are honest with ourselves, we have to admit that this kind of pride may have little to do with good character. After we have died, the importance of such things will fade. They will become like black and white movies, locked into a time that is over. Trophies get pushed to the back of a display cabinet, new presidents take over corporations, and important possessions need repairs. However, the man we become—our character and faith—and the things that we achieve by faith, these things will last.

If we ask ourselves what reason can we give to make our sons proud, we need to reach beyond the predictable. We want something that will last.

Know Your Purpose and Pursue It With All Your Might

Years ago, God placed in my heart the desire to reach men in high places with the gospel of Christ. I saw myself not so much as an evangelist as a matchmaker, introducing men to the God of the Universe. Many times I would go downtown at 4 o'clock in the morning and pray outside the headquarters of major corporations. I must have been a strange sight in the dark, walking the streets and sometimes kneeling to pray. I would drive to our international airport and get out of my car to pray for those who would pass through our city in the coming hours of the morning to conduct business. God gave me a burden for this and I have embraced it with all of my heart. By faith I knew He was calling me to have an impact on men and that sports would play an important role.

God rewards those who seek Him, and He has rewarded me in ways I cannot begin to explain. Many, many unusual and remarkable opportunities have come to me as a result of those prayers, and I have been privileged to speak about Christ to many men in positions of influence and power. Because I understood my calling and pursued it, I knew what doors to walk through. God has given me a position as chaplain of an NBA team. I also lead Pro Athletes Outreach, a Seattle organization started in 1971 that has helped thousands of athletes successfully deal with the pressures of pro sports.

If I had listened to the counsel of some people, I would have never started down this path. I would have played it safe and gotten a job I could explain, with regular hours. But that is not what God had for me. I have tried to listen in prayer to his counsel, and this is where he has directed me. Though my path is unconventional, I believe God calls me to pursue it with all of my might. That is your challenge as well, to do what God has given you to do with all of your might.

When you live by faith, you become a Bible that your son can read. Your life becomes proof that God is real. The same God who appeared in a burning bush to Moses is the God who is *with you*. He is *in you*. He is *right now*. He will direct you to do things that bring him glory—things that require faith. As your son matures and begins to live his own life of trusting God, your life of faith will give him a reason to be proud. It will encourage him and bless him, giving him a pride that won't fluctuate with the stock market or look shabby with age. It will grow brighter with time. Try to imagine what it will be like for your son, as an old man, to put his grandson on his lap and tell him of the faith lessons he learned from you when he was a child. The company you started or the size of your home will seem of little importance by comparison.

Daddy, I want to encourage you to know your purpose and to pursue it with all of your might. To live like this means you will do things you have not done before. Sometimes, God will ask things of you that won't make sense. Be willing to listen; be willing to act. The result will be something you could never have orchestrated, but which will make a lasting impression on your children.

Living By Faith

One Sunday morning, during our minivan years, I was on the way to church with Loretta and the children. As I headed toward the interstate, I got a feeling that we shouldn't be going to church. By the time I was on the highway, the feeling had become strong. Knowing how peculiar my words would sound, I turned to Loretta and told her.

"Loretta, I think we need to go back home. I think this needs to be a day when we just"—I felt strange hearing myself say the words—"that we just turn around and go back home." Immediately my children started objecting—they love church and they love their friends. But Loretta was okay with it, so I turned around and headed home. My kids were not happy.

I soon found myself behind a lady in a station wagon —you don't see many of those anymore. We were driving 60 miles an hour when suddenly her tire blew out. It happened right in front of us, and I braked. She pulled over on the shoulder, so as I passed her, I pulled over in front of her. By the time I got out of my car, she was standing by her car, nervously smoking a cigarette.

To fully appreciate this picture, you have to understand that I don't know anything about mechanics. I can fix a tire but it takes me twice as long as anybody who knows what they are doing.

I introduced myself and asked if she had a cell phone.

"No, I don't," she answered. I held out mine. "Why don't you call your husband and tell him that my name is Perry, that I'm a black man, and then give him my license plate number."

She didn't know what to do, especially when I said, 'black man.'

"I don't have to do that, I really—I mean, I don't . . ." she faltered, not knowing what to say.

"Listen," I told her, "if this happened to my wife, I hope a man would say the very thing that I am saying to you. So just call anybody. And I'm going to look in your trunk and make sure I can get everything out." Reluctantly, she took the phone and I walked back to the car. I got the spare tire out and the jack, the old-fashioned kind that you pump by hand.

I glanced up at her, now some distance away, puffing on her cigarette. "Lord, help me," I silently prayed. This was not going to be easy.

After setting up the jack, I stood up and spoke to her. "Excuse me, ma'am—my wife is up there. Why don't you go introduce yourself to her? And to my children?" With that she turned and walked towards the van. "God," I began to pray, struggling with the lugs, "God you know that I'm not very good with this stuff. Either you're going to have to fix this tire or she needs Jesus. So, if she needs you right now, would you give me the opportunity to tell her about you?"

The minutes ticked by as I struggled to change the tire. The woman came back to check on me, working on another cigarette. When she got close to the car I looked up at her. I wasn't making much progress.

"Ma'am, can I ask you a personal question?" I said. "Were you afraid?"

"I was so *scared*," she answered, shaking her head. "I was so scared because of how the car jerked."

"I saw it, I was behind you," I said, pausing to give her time to think through how she felt. I had something else I wanted to bring up.

"Let me ask you this question," I continued. "What would have happened if you had lost control and there had been an ugly wreck? And you had been killed?" She didn't say anything. She was troubled.

"On a scale from zero to ten, if something tragic had happened—if you had died—how sure are you that you would go to heaven?" I gently asked.

She looked at me. "A two," she answered.

My heart went out to her. "How would you like to be a five? To have that much certainty?"

Hesitating, she said, "I'm not that good."

To her, a "five" was a stretch. So I pushed further. "How would you like to be an eight or a nine?"

No more hesitating now. "I'm not *that* good!" she said firmly.

She had probably never had a conversation like this before. "I just want you to know that even an eight or a nine can't do it. If there was a wreck—a fatal accident and you were killed—you have to be a ten. And the only way you can be a ten is that you've got to believe that Jesus is the Son of God."

She was listening intently now. I began to talk to her about the gospel. After a few minutes, I could see she wanted to become a Christian. Dropping her cigarette and crushing it with her shoe, she held out her hand to pray with me to receive Christ. We bowed our heads on the side of the highway, cars rushing by as we prayed.

"Amen," I said, opening my eyes. I looked at her and asked, "Do you believe that you are a Christian?" With confidence she smiled and said, "I do!"

"I want you to look at something," I told her.

She followed my eyes, which were now on the van. Up the highway, on the shoulder, I could see my kids going crazy inside. I could tell they were jumping around, and it looked like they were hollering, "Yeeeesssss!"

"What are they doing?" the lady asked.

"They are so happy that you gave your life to Jesus Christ. Go and tell them," I said.

As she left, I returned to the flat tire and in minutes, it was fixed. Everything fell into place.

We said our goodbyes and got back into our cars. At the first exit I turned around and headed towards church. Now I understood. God wasn't saying, "Don't go." He was saying, "Don't go *yet*."

I think our children need to see us succeed in the way we

live our lives. The very thing that we talk about in our homes, about following Christ, should be happening as we live. May they see us listening for God's directions on the highway of life and having the faith to trust Him with what we hear. Our sons need new stories about our great God. As we live by faith, these fresh stories get written into their lives.

What they read about God in the Bible becomes the same as what they see about God in our lives.

People Will Learn About a Father From His Son

In the years ahead, your son will reveal what kind of father you have been. If someone meets him at work or in his neighborhood, on the golf course or in a classroom, they will eventually begin to hear about you. It's natural for a man to talk about his father and the influence he has had on his life.

David never lost his reputation as the "son of Jesse." Throughout his life, people both greeted him and insulted him by invoking his father's name. Saul, in fury, called him "the son of Jesse" when angrily confronting Jonathan about their friendship (I Samuel 20:30). Nabal, a surly but wealthy man who refused David's request for help, asked, "Who is this David? Who is this son of Jesse?" (I Samuel 25:10). His words ring with contempt. David, however, treasured and held on to his identity as Jesse's son, even when he became old. At the end of his life, when he wrote his last song, his signature read, "David the son of Jesse" (II Samuel 23:1). His final prayers were followed by this note: "The prayers of David the son of Jesse are ended" (Psalm 72:20). To the end, we see in David a man who was identified by his father.

The pages of the Old Testament closed with a promise, that God would send a new son of Jesse. This man would emerge out of a family line so severely cut back that only a stump would remain. Yet if the Jews wanted to know where to look for the Messiah, they could look to the root of Jesse. "The Spirit of the Lord will rest on him," Isaiah wrote (11:2). This man—this Messiah—would have insight, he would have power, and he would know God. This son of Jesse, foreshadowed by David, would be the son who would rule forever.

At the heart of the gospel is the love between a father and his son. The story of the House of Jesse is the seed that explodes into a towering oak, becoming the New Testament story of a son who left his father's house in heaven to become the king on earth. In our Lord we meet a son who learned what his father taught him and did what his father asked of him. As he told his friends a few days before his death, "Everything that I learned from my Father I have made known to you" (John 15:15).

At every point in the lessons we have learned about the House of Jesse, we see parallels in the life of Christ. Our story began with teaching our sons *to not judge by outward appearances*, and I shared with you about my brother, Eddie. When we look at Christ, we see the ultimate son who did not judge by outward appearances. He showed no favoritism to the wealthy and he told stories, like that of the Good Samaritan, which confronted prejudice. Isaiah foretold about him: "He will not judge by what he sees with his eyes, or decide by what he hears with his ears" (Isaiah 11:3). As the Contemporary English Version puts it: "This king won't judge by appearances or listen to rumors."

Like David, Christ *obeyed* his father out of love. "I love the Father and … I do exactly what my Father has commanded me" (John 14:31). But he had to learn this obedience, and it came through suffering. Just as David returned again and again to take care of his father's flock, choosing obedience over joining the army and fighting, so also Christ patiently cared for his father's flock, resisting the temptation to join legions of angels at his command to fight Satan. He obeyed his father and did not take matters into his own hands. "Although he was a son, he learned obedience from what he suffered" (Hebrews 5:8).

Jesus also was a son who *gave comfort*. "Do not let your hearts be troubled," he told the disciples. "I will come back and take you to be with me" (John 14:1, 3). He knew how to speak words that would bring strength. He had insight into the thoughts that troubled his friends' hearts. He knew what to say.

Our Lord was *properly instructed* and *equipped* for his task. His ministry began with a severe temptation in the desert that included personal conversations with Satan. Jesus was ready for this test, having waited until he was thirty years old to begin his public ministry. He was also properly instructed to recognize the role of others. He waited for his cousin John to fully develop his ministry before he came to him to be baptized. He knew John's role was to "prepare the way," just as the Old Testament had prophesied.

The Jews wanted a *champion* who was a military hero, someone who would defeat the Romans, but Christ showed them that a *true hero is a man of faith.* "I lay down my life for the sheep," he said, preparing for the cross (John 10:15). By faith, he faced an enemy larger than Goliath: he battled Death and won. His victory became our hope. Just as he was raised from the dead, so we have been raised with him, to live a new life.

Another parallel we see is that the Father gave his son *a reason to come home.* "In my Father's house are many rooms . . . I am going there to prepare a place for you," Christ said (John 14:1, 2). "If you loved me you would be glad that I am going to the Father" he told his followers (v. 28). He looked forward to returning to his home, and he planned to get it ready for his friends. At his Father's house, there was room for everyone. It was a place to look forward to.

We also see in Christ a son who was *responsible.* When misunderstood, he explained himself. When blamed for causing trouble, he took responsibility. When he saw something immoral, he addressed it. When exhausted, he continued to minister. When faced with dull students, he taught patiently. He did not define himself by the failures of others, nor did he quit when he faced obstacles. He assumed responsibility to teach, heal, rebuke, and love and was not deterred or discouraged from his mission.

And like David, Christ knew how to *encourage* others. He understood the heart issues and addressed them. Just as David had insight into the fears of those who faced Goliath, so Christ had insight into the fears that held back the people around him. He knew Peter so well, for example, that he prepared him for the self-recrimination that would follow his denial. On the one hand, Christ predicted he would deny him under pressure. On the other, he assured him, "I have prayed for you, Simon, that your faith may not fail. And when you have turned back, strengthen your brothers" (Luke 22:32). Peter's faith would waver, but it would not, ultimately, fail. Christ knew exactly what to tell Peter to protect his hope.

Just as David killed the threats to his flock—the *lion and the bear*—so also the Lord Jesus wrestled with the predators that attacked his sheep. In the garden of Gethsemane he challenged his friends to stay awake and not give in to a lazy attitude. "Then he came to the disciples and found them sleeping, and said to Peter, 'What! Could you not watch with me one hour?'" (Mt 26:40 NKJV). He warned his followers to "watch and pray" and not to be lulled to sleep by a false sense of peace. Our Savior also destroyed the bear of the past for every believer. Paul wrote, "if anyone is in Christ, he is a new creation; the old has gone, the new has come!" (II Corinthians 5:17) Whatever accusation the Devil wants to make against us, he must first make it against Christ. Our past is gone and our new life is in him. As Paul explained it, "you have died and your life is hidden with Christ in God" (Colossians 3:3).

Finally, Jesus was *proud* to call God his father. "I have come in my Father's name," he declared with pride (John 5:43). "I honor my Father," he said (John 8:49). He had a father who both knew him and loved him, things he openly claimed and talked about (John 10:15, 17).

"Those Who Honor Me I Will Honor" (I Samuel 2:30)
Our Lord was so confident about his similarity to his father that he could tell others, "If you really knew me, you

would know my Father as well" (John 14:7). There was an unmistakable likeness. "He has told us about him," John wrote (John 1:18 NLT). Jesus claimed that the things he said came directly from his father. In a private conversation with his disciples at the end of his life, he told them, "whatever I say is just what the Father has told me to say" (John 14:24). He copied what he saw his father doing, claiming that his dad loved him and let him in on his business. "Whatever the Father does the Son also does. For the Father loves the Son and shows him all he does" (John 5:19-20). Jesus emulated his father because he loved him. He obeyed him in everything.

Jesus was so confident of being like his father that he told people to not believe him unless they could tell he acted like his dad. "Do not believe me unless I do what my Father does" (John 10:37). Everything we have learned about Jesse and David points to a father and son relationship that is bigger than anything we could imagine. It inspires us to become not only better fathers, but to become a son like Christ. Ultimately, the House of Jesse is not just about being a father like Jesse, it is also about becoming a son like our Savior.

Daddy, my blessing to you as we close this study is that you would raise your sons to be like David and that you would shape them to become giant killers. As you honor God, he will honor you. But I desire an even greater blessing for you. As you follow the Lord Jesus Christ—the ultimate son whose story was foreshadowed by the House of Jesse—I pray that you will become a son of Jesse yourself.

A king asked David to tell him about his father. May the great men of our generation ask you the same.

"Tell me about your father, my boy."

Contact Information for Perry Tuttle

P.O. Box 78241
Charlotte, NC 28271

email: perry@perrytuttle.com
perrytuttle.com